First Aid for Cats

First published in Australia in 2007 by
New Holland Publishers (Australia) Pty Ltd
Sydney • Auckland • London • Cape Town

14 Aquatic Drive Frenchs Forest NSW 2086 Australia
218 Lake Road Northcote Auckland New Zealand
86 Edgware Road London W2 2EA United Kingdom
80 McKenzie Street Cape Town 8001 South Africa

National Library of Australia Cataloguing-in-Publication Data:
Wimpole, Justin.
        First aid for cats.

        Includes index.
        ISBN: 978-1-74110-475-2

        1. Cats - Wounds and injuries - Treatment. 2. Cats -
        Diseases - Treatment. 3. First aid for animals - Handbooks,
        manuals, etc. I. Title.

        636.8089710262

Publisher: Fiona Schultz
Project Editor: Michael McGrath
Editor: Jenny Scepanovic
Production: Linda Bottari
Printer: McPherson's Printing Group, Victoria
Cover Image: Photolibrary

First Aid for Cats

By Dr Justin Wimpole BVSc (hons)

NEW HOLLAND

Acknowledgments

I am fortunate to have had a lot of people encourage me to write this book and they all deserve my gratitude.

Firstly, I am most appreciative of the support provided by my partner, Kate, who is also a veterinarian and provided the illustrations. My parents, Helena and Denis, and my brother Martin have also always been full of praise and encouragement. Kate's family, especially Roger, has also been very supportive.

It would be remiss of me not to express my gratitude and admiration for my feline friend Beetle and canine companion Milo, who were present for almost every word I wrote and provided unconditional affection.

My friends are also an endless source of motivation. My colleagues at the Veterinary Specialist Centre continue to provide me with inspiration.

I thank Fiona Schultz and the staff at New Holland and my agents Xavier Waterkeyn and Clare Calvert at Flying Pigs for their support. Finally and most importantly, I would like to thank all of my patients who continue to stimulate me and teach me new things every day.

Contents

Introduction

Cats are very special creatures that play a unique role in our lives. Human populations tend to attract rodents—and hence cats—so cats have been drawn to us to form a mutually beneficial relationship that remains to this day. There is evidence of the domestic cat living with humans in ancient Egyptian times and possibly even earlier. The importance of the cat's role as a rodent hunter is accentuated by the bubonic plague, which was spread by fleas on rats and resulted in the death of one quarter of Europe's human population. Domestic cats played a role in bringing the rodent population under control, stemming the spread of disease.

The way that cats relate to humans has essentially not changed throughout history. Evidence to support this is the fact that although there are many different breeds of domestic cat, they are very similar in size; the well-defined role that cats play means that humans have not had to select heavily for specific characteristics. This is very different when it comes to dogs, where people have created various breeds of dog that vary vastly in size and shape for more specific roles.

Contrary to popular opinion, cats can be very social animals. Some wild cats including lions and cheetahs do live socially. Similarly, the domestic cat can live with other cats, people and dogs. Cats are often seen as animals that tolerate people because of the benefits we provide them rather than actually living with us for our companionship; this is why people often say that 'dogs have owners, cats have staff'. However, domestic cats are not simply living with humans because of the nutritional benefits they provide, loving relationships exist between cats and people and these bonds can be extremely strong. Domesticated cats are able to become feral and live independently of people but so often choose not to and are often bonded to specific individuals — other cats, dogs or people — and can be very loyal.

Although cats are are normally perfectly able to look after themselves and give back to us at least as much as we give them, when they are sick or injured they are completely dependent on us. When this is the case we want to do whatever we can to help them. There are many hazards for our feline friends, but we may feel helpless or ill prepared to be of any assistance. Adding to the challenge, cats are especially good at hiding their illnesses and often by the time they are showing signs of severe illness their condition is quite advanced. Also cats do not always like being examined and treated, even when they are well. These issues can make administering first aid and veterinary care to cats difficult. Fortunately there are 24-hour emergency animal health centres in most capital cities and regional centres. Most areas have veterinarians who provide after-hours service on a call-out basis. In most cases the best thing that you can do for a sick or injured cat is to seek prompt veterinary attention for professional assessment and access to diagnostic testing and timely treatment.

Unfortunately not all cat owners have access to veterinary attention at all times. This book provides some basic information to cat owners and carers to help them avoid an emergency, recognise an emergency and better equip them to act appropriately. It by no means aims to replace or delay veterinary assistance. Treating it as such is dangerous and could put your cat's life at risk. You should only intervene when it is imperative that something is done immediately, when you have no access to veterinary attention or when veterinary attention is far away. Sometimes an owner can save their cat's life by giving appropriate first aid.

When I provide veterinary attention to animals, I always attempt to apply the philosophy of 'do no harm'. The information in this book is presented with this principle in mind. Unfortunately when owners or even veterinarians try to help a sick or injured cat, there is the potential to do more harm. This is obviously not intentional. It is imperative that first aid given to a sick or injured cat helps the cat's situation rather than making it worse.

By reading this book to better equip yourself for emergencies involving your cat, you are showing a real commitment to your companion. Hopefully you will never need to use the information presented in this book, but should the need arise you will be better equipped to deal with the situation.

Disclaimer

This book was written to offer cat owners and lovers first aid advice on dealing with emergencies involving cats. The advice is general in nature.

It was written using veterinary knowledge and experience, but should never be used as a substitute for professional assessment, advice or care. In some instances providing first aid has the potential to cause harm to the patient and the person providing it. It is the responsibility of the reader to consider these risks when deciding on a course of action in any particular situation. Readers should be aware that, even with the benefit of a veterinary hospital setting, the outcome of emergency situations can be undesirable including permanent injury or loss of life. Results can be expected to be even less successful in the field situation.

The author and publisher cannot be held responsible for any loss or personal injury caused by the application of any advice provided in this book.

If in doubt, please contact your nearest veterinary hospital immediately.

Being Prepared

The most important aspect of being prepared for an animal emergency is to have a good relationship with your veterinarian. You can easily achieve this simply by attending to your cat's routine preventative medical requirements, such as having your cat vaccinated and examined regularly. With regular consultations you will learn about flea control, intestinal worm and heartworm prevention, diet and other aspects of caring for your cat. Seeing your veterinarian regularly will also allow them to identify and manage your cat's individual issues and be aware of them in case of an emergency.

Know your local veterinary surgery's opening hours. Talk to your veterinarian about provisions for after-hours emergencies. Some provide their own emergency service as required. Where this type of service is provided some clinics will have live-in staff. Other clinics divert their emergencies to another clinic close by. A group of clinics may share the after-hours service on a roster. Some nights or weekends it will be your regular clinic, otherwise it will be another clinic close by. Some clinics send their after-hours emergencies to a dedicated emergency centre. Often when a veterinary clinic has a critical patient that requires 24-hour care, they may elect to send them to such a service for ongoing monitoring and treatment overnight.

When you call your regular veterinary surgery's number after hours you may speak to someone directly; however, there will more likely be clear recorded instructions, perhaps providing the number of a pager or another hospital, and where to take your animal. So you are best prepared for an emergency it is important to know what arrangements your particular veterinary surgery has, preferably before you have an emergency situation. After-hours services of all types are usually significantly more expensive than those during regular surgery hours. So if you think that your cat is unwell during normal surgery hours it is much more economical (and much less stressful) to see your regular veterinarian during normal surgery hours rather than see a veterinarian that you do not know after hours when your cat's condition may have progressed. Expedient assessment and treatment is also obviously better for your cat.

Keep a readily accessible record of this information as well as other important details and phone numbers. There is a space for you to record this information under Emergency Contacts on page 111.

Knowing your veterinarian's regular surgery hours: what type of after-hours service is provided and where you should go in an after-hours emergency, is very important.

Unfortunately there is no organised animal ambulance service available at all times. One common obstacle owners have in an emergency is transport. If you do not have a car then knowing what emergency services are available is especially important. Emergency centres may be much further than your regular veterinary clinic. Some veterinarians provide a house call service; however, this is not always available after hours. If you do not have access to a car or an ambulatory veterinary service you will have to arrange alternative transport. Several pet transport services are available in metropolitan areas, but many do not operate after hours. Most taxi companies will transport cats. Exactly which company will do this is something that you will have to investigate in your area. In an emergency you should specify to the taxi company that you wish to transport a sick animal so that they can send a willing driver. Often owners have to rely on neighbours and friends to provide transport for them and their cat in an emergency situation if they do not have their own transport

This book provides basic advice on how to help your cat if they are sick or injured. However, it is very beneficial to understand your cat as well as you can and be as aware as possible of what is normal for them when they are well.

History

The more you know about your cat's routine when it's well, the better chance you have of detecting subtle changes which may indicate disease. Things to note are your cat's thirst, appetite, diet, urination and defecation habits. Monitor your cat's water intake and note any changes. The amount of water that cats consume varies markedly among individuals, largely due to different amounts of water in their diets. Cats eating mostly dry food usually drink more. Other cats may hardly drink at all. Generally, if a cat drinks more than 50mL of water per kilogram of body weight, this is considered excessive.

Changes in your cat's appetite may indicate illness. Reduced appetite is a common but non-specific sign of many feline diseases (see page 60). On the other hand, an increased appetite may indicate a problem like diabetes (see page 96) or hyperthyroidism (see page 103).

Excessive volumes of urine may indicate diabetes (see page 96) or a kidney problem (see page 100). Increased frequency or urination in unusual areas, straining or difficulty urinating, bloody or foul smelling urine may indicate a lower urinary tract disorder (see page 69). Inability to pass urine, especially in males, may indicate a urinary obstruction, which is a medical emergency (see page 70). Note your cat's defecation, including: frequency, whether their stool is normally formed, overly large and dry, or diarrhea. Note straining to defecate, which may indicate constipation or inflammation of the large bowel or colitis (see page 65) or the presence of blood or mucus.

Physical examination

Owners who learn to perform a basic physical examination on their cat are better prepared to help them if they become sick. The more your veterinarian knows about your animal's condition, the better equipped they are to help.

Know your cat's normal gum colour, heart and pulse rates, breathing patterns and temperature. Practise observing and measuring these things. It is your best chance of detecting a problem if it becomes unwell.

Gum colour

Your cat's gum colour and that of the roof of its mouth are things that you can check easily. Simply lift your cat's upper lip or gently pull down on the lower lip and observe the colour of the gums or the inner lip. To look at the roof of its mouth use one hand to hold its head by its cheekbones on either side and use the index or middle finger of the other hand to open the lower jaw (careful not to get bitten). The normal gum colour and that of the roof of the mouth of a cat varies a little but is usually a healthy pink.

Pale pink or white gums may indicate anaemia (low red blood cell counts), pain or shock (see Assessing the Feline Emergency Patient on page 41). Yellow or jaundiced gums may indicate liver problems, blockage of bile flow or excessive breakdown of red blood cells. Either way, pale to

Examining a cat's gums and the roof of its mouth.

whitish or yellowish gums usually indicate severe illness. Brownish gums may also indicate paracetamol toxicity (see Poisoning on page 74), and greyish gums can indicate severe ill health. Some cats have naturally pigmented or black areas of the gums so it is important to know what is normal when your cat is well.

Some conditions, such as serious infections, will make the gums brick red. Poor blood oxygen levels can cause the gums to have a bluish tinge. Excessively red gums can indicate gingivitis and these gums may bleed easily. Bruising to the gums may indicate trauma or a problem with blood clotting. Oozing of blood from the gums can also indicate a blood clotting problem.

You may also notice excessive dental tartar build up on the teeth. Bad breath is often associated with dental disease but it can also occur with pneumonia, kidney problems (see Kidney Problems on page 100) or diabetic ketosis (see Diabetes on page 99). In some conditions such as so-called cat flu (see Sneezing, Snifflles and Snuffles on page 92) or kidney problems you may notice ulcers in the mouth or on the tongue. If your cat's gums and mouth are excessively dry or tacky, this can indicate dehydration.

Heart rate

Another aspect of your cat's health you can monitor is its heart rate. The easiest way to do this without a stethoscope is to feel for the heartbeat on the chest wall. You can feel this best on the left-hand side of the chest just behind the left elbow, either while the cat is standing or lying on its side.

Count the number of beats in 15 seconds and multiply this by four to find the number of beats per minute. A cat's normal resting heart rate is about 140–180 beats per minute. This should be measured when your cat is calm and resting. An excited or frightened cat can have a heart rate up to 220 beats per minute. Illness can also affect a cat's heart rate.

Feeling a cat's chest for a heartbeat.

Pulse rate

The pulse rate is usually but not always the same as the heart rate. The best way to measure your cat's pulse rate is to measure the femoral pulse. This is located on the inner surface of the thigh. This is a little more difficult to locate than the heartbeat and may require more practice. You can most easily find this when your cat is standing, by standing behind it and reaching in front of its thigh and gently feeling for the pulse high up on the inner surface of its thigh. Using your index and middle fingers, feel for a groove running down the leg in the middle of the inner thigh where the large blood vessels run. You can also feel for this when it is lying on its side.

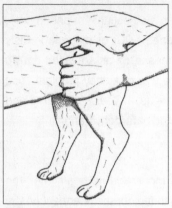

Feeling for the femoral pulse.

It can be difficult to judge the quality of the pulse, but if you are familiar with your cat's pulse when it is well, you are more likely to be able to describe it when it is unwell. For example it can be weak, normal or bounding.

Breathing

Your cat's rate of breathing and the effort that it needs to put into breathing also tells you something about your cat's health. At rest your cat's breathing rate should be around 8–32 breaths per minute; however, many factors will influence this. Your cat should breathe with minimal effort with only the chest wall moving for the most part.

When cats are having difficulty breathing the breathing rate will increase and the chest movements will become laboured and exaggerated.

As a cat becomes more distressed, it starts breathing with its belly as well as its chest. If the problem is an upper airway obstruction its breathing may also be noisy. Cats that are having difficulty breathing may be restless, reluctant to lie down and unable to sleep. Cats normally only breathe through their nose. If they are in severe respiratory distress or if they are extremely stressed they may start open mouth breathing or panting. Cats that are having severe difficulty breathing may also stand with their forelimbs apart and their head and neck stretched out.

Any difficulty breathing while your cat is completely at rest represents a true emergency. Bear in mind that it is easy to underestimate how much difficulty a cat is having to breathe. Once you notice that a cat is having difficulty breathing, it is likely that it is in significant respiratory distress and it needs to see a veterinarian immediately.

Body temperature

Changes in body temperature may indicate hypothermia, overheating or fever. A cat's normal body temperature is higher than a human's, so cats will usually feel warm to touch. This is normal but often mistaken for a fever. A cat's temperature is most accurately measured rectally. You need someone to hold the cat while you check this. Use either a glass or a digital thermometer. You should shake down glass thermometers before use. The tips of either type of thermometer should be lubricated, preferably with water-based lubricant. You then carefully insert the thermometer directly into the anus 1–2 cm. Then gently angle it to one side so that the tip of the thermometer is up against the rectal wall. A common mistake is to leave the tip of the thermometer in the centre of the rectum, often within a stool. This measures the temperature of the faeces rather than the core body temperature.

Glass analogue thermometers need to be in place for around two minutes before you read them. Be careful not to break a glass thermometer while it is in your cat's rectum, especially if your cat is struggling. Digital thermometers are generally faster and usually beep once they have finished measuring. A cat's normal temperature is around 37.5–39.5°C. Many factors influence your cat's body temperature including the temperature of the room, the weather and any activity your cat has been doing. You should take these factors into consideration when measuring body temperature. If the temperature is only just outside the normal range, consider repeating the measurement say after an hour or two to verify that a problem exists.

Because all cats are individuals and vary slightly, if you have more than one cat, you need to practise taking measurements on each of them and become familiar with what is normal for each individual.

- Normal gum colour of a cat should be a healthy pink.
- Normal resting pulse rate of a cat is 140–180 beats per minute.
- Cats normally breathe through their nose with minimal effort with a resting breathing rate of 8–32 breaths per minute.
- Normal rectal temperature of a cat is 37.5–39.5°C.

Your Feline First Aid Kit

A feline first aid kit need only contain some very basic supplies for an emergency. One of the most important items in this kit should be your veterinarian's name and contact details. It should include details of surgery hours and after-hours arrangements. You should also have the details of at least one veterinary emergency centre near you that is open after hours.

You should have the number for the council ranger. During office hours, you can usually contact the ranger through the appropriate council's main line. Some larger councils will have a 24-hour emergency service and the ranger can be contacted through an after-hours number. However, other councils only have a ranger service during normal business hours. You should have also have an easily accessed record that lists the number of a poisons information centre and other important phone numbers. There is a space for you to record this information under Emergency Contacts on page 111.

Δ

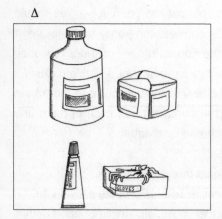 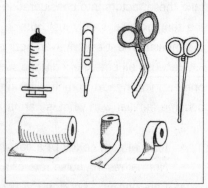

Clockwise from top left: sterile saline, gauze swabs, syringe, digital thermometer, scissors, tape, conforming gauze, adhesive bandage, gloves and Betadine® ointment.

The most important items you need in your feline first aid kit are:

Saline
This can be sterile saline purchased from a pharmacy or your veterinarian. Saline is primarily used for bathing or flushing wounds. It can also be used to flush the eyes. Alternatively saline can be made by dissolving 3 teaspoons of table salt in a litre of water. This is not as good as it is not a sterile solution, but it is acceptable in an emergency situation.

Large syringe
This should be at least 20 ml and does not need to have a needle attached. Syringes are available from a pharmacy or your veterinarian. This can be used to draw up the saline and inject it into wounds to flush them out. Saline from a syringe can be used to carefully flush the eyes when they have been contaminated with an irritating substance. You can use a syringe to give your cat some water if you feel that it is dehydrated or is not drinking enough. Smaller syringes are also useful for giving liquid medications orally and occasionally rectally.

Non-adherent dressings
Cotton and cloth bandages will adhere to open wounds and make removing the bandages very painful and difficult. Non-adherent dressings can be applied to open wounds to prevent this from happening. A soft dressing is then applied on top of the non-adherent dressing.

Roll-cotton dressing
This is used to bandage wounds and is available in various widths. It holds the non-adherent dressing against the wound and also absorbs secretions such as blood, discharge and bacteria taking them away from the wound. It will also serve to partially immobilise the area and pads the wound, protecting it from further trauma. This provides even pressure and helps prevent the other layers of bandage from digging in too much.

Conforming gauze dressing

This is used over roll-cotton dressings to help hold the bandage in place and give some degree of firmness. Conforming gauze can be either rigid or have some degree of elasticity and is available in various widths. I prefer products with some elasticity.

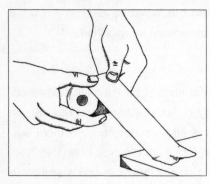

Unrolling and re-rolling adhesive bandage.

Adhesive bandage

This is used over the gauze bandage to hold the whole dressing in place. Because these types of bandages are very sticky they can be difficult to unravel. This means that they are difficult to apply without inadvertently making them too tight. To avoid this, before you apply such bandages you should unravel them completely and then re-roll them.

Tape

There are many different types of tape you can use to help hold bandages or splints in place. You can also use tape with cotton wool or gauze to make bandaids. When you use tape you should fold the free end on itself to make a little tab. This will make it far easier to remove. The best type for your kit is probably a clear tape that is not too sticky rather than a very adhesive cloth tape that is harder to remove.

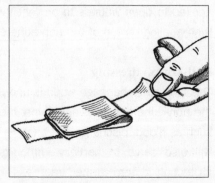

Using gauze to make a bandaid.

Gauze swabs

These are square pieces of gauze that are available in various sizes. They are useful for wiping and cleaning or to apply pressure to areas of bleeding. You can also fold them up and use these with some tape to create bandaids for your cat.

Thermometer
These can be glass or digital and should only be used rectally. Digital thermometers are much more convenient, quicker and easier to use and read.

Water-based lubricant
This is required to lubricate the tip of the thermometer before use. You can also use sterile water-based lubricant (from a previously unopened sterile tube) to fill open wounds before applying a dressing. This helps to prevent contamination with hair and dirt.

Tick removers
The major types of tick removers are ones with a forceps or tweezer-like action, one that hooks under the tick and one that uses a small lasso. These work using a twisting action. Any of these are acceptable; however, I find the ones that hook under the tick are easier to use. You can purchase these from your veterinarian or a pet shop.

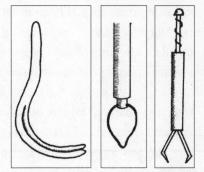

From left: hook, lasso and tweezer-type tick removers.

Scissors
These are useful for cutting bandages and tapes. They should have rounded tips to avoid cutting your cat while using them near him or her.

Tweezers or forceps
These can be useful to remove small objects embedded in your cat's skin such as obvious splinters, small pieces of glass, insect stings, ticks or grass seeds. Anything other than these needs to be removed by your veterinarian.

Gloves

Latex examination gloves are not sterile; however, they help to reduce contamination of wounds with the natural bacteria on your hands. They also protect you from coming into contact with blood and other body fluid.

Hydrogen peroxide

You can use a 3 per cent solution to safely induce vomiting. Most preparations available from the supermarket or pharmacy are this concen-tration. You need to dilute more concentrated solutions to 3 per cent. For example, if you have a 10 per cent solution you can use one part of this solution to two parts water to make approximately a 3 per cent solution (see Poisoning on page 74).

Soda crystals

Crystals of sodium carbonate can be useful for inducing vomiting and are very safe. You can purchase them from a pharmacy or a supermarket in the laundry section. However, it can be very difficult to administer adequate amounts of soda crystals to a cat, so hydrogen peroxide is often a better option. (see Poisoning on page 74)

Activated charcoal tablets or solution

Activated charcoal can sometimes be useful to bind poisons in the gut that your cat has ingested. You can purchase these from a pharmacy (see Poisoning on page 74).

Betadine® (povidone iodine 10 per cent) solution or ointment

This is a relatively safe iodine-based antiseptic solution that may be helpful, for example when bathing the umbilical cord of newly born kittens. Betadine® ointment can also be used on bandaids as an antiseptic. You should not use other antiseptics such as Dettol® as they can be very harmful to cats' skin. No antiseptic should be left in contact with the skin for prolonged periods.

Any medications that your cat has been prescribed for an emergency situation should be included in your kit. For example, if your cat requires heart medication it may have been prescribed additional diuretics to be administered in an emergency situation. If your cat is diabetic it is important to have a source of sugar easily available such as honey or corn syrup. There is further advice on how to use these items throughout this book.

Painkillers and NSAIDs

You will notice that I have not included any pain or fever relief medications in the first aid kit. The majority of pain relief medications used in cats are either non-steroidal anti-inflammatory drugs (NSAIDs) like aspirin or opioids such as morphine. As is the case with all drugs, NSAIDs not only have beneficial effects but can also have negative side effects including stomach ulcers and kidney damage. Cats are especially sensitive to these side effects. These effects can be exacerbated in certain circumstances, particularly if your cat is dehydrated (see Dehydration on page 64). Some medications will interact with NSAIDs and they should not be given concurrently. For these reasons I do not recommend that you keep NSAIDs in your cat's first aid kit. NSAIDs recommended by your veterinarian for use in cats are much safer and easier to dose accurately than those registered for humans. If your cat has been prescribed an NSAID you may be able to use this in an emergency situation if your veterinarian has given you guidelines to do so.

Although opioids are relatively safe and very effective painkillers when used properly, they are rarely prescribed for use at home as they are highly regulated drugs and often need to be given by injection. Paracetamol is an over-the-counter drug that people often take for pain relief. Cats are extremely sensitive to paracetamol and can easily be poisoned by it. Paracetamol toxicity is discussed in Poisoning on page 74.

DO NOT GIVE YOUR CAT PARACETAMOL—EVER.

Giving cats tablets

Administering tablets and other medications to cats can be challenging. Sometimes cats will eat medication in their food but often they will either pick it out or will not eat food with medication in it. Cats will also learn when you are about to give medication and will either run away and hide or very quickly become aggressive. Generally it is best to be as quick as possible because your first chance is your best and this minimises stress for you and your cat. The easiest way I find to give a cat a tablet is as follows:

Using the middle finger to pull down lower jaw.

1. Take the tablet in you preferred hand between your thumb and forefinger. Use your non-preferred hand to grasp your cat's head holding onto the cheekbones on each side. You can also use your elbow of this arm to help stop your cat backing up away from you.

2. Use the middle finger of your preferred hand to open your cat's mouth by carefully but firmly pulling down on its lower jaw.

Putting the tablet as far back in the cat's mouth as possible.

3. Quickly place the tablet as far back in your cat's mouth as possible and then hold its mouth shut for a few seconds. Be careful to avoid being bitten.

4. Unless your cat eats immediately after receiving a tablet or capsule, it is always a good idea to administer 2–5 mL of water via a syringe to wash it down out of its oesophagus or food pipe and into its stomach. This is especially important for certain medications so you should discuss this with your veterinarian.

When a cat has swallowed a tablet it will usually lick its nose. Sometimes smearing a small amount of butter or margarine on the tablet or capsule can help your cat swallow it, especially if it is a large tablet. So-called pill-poppers that you can buy from your veterinarian can be beneficial in helping you get the pill as far back into the cat's mouth as possible.

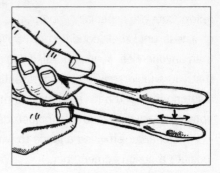

Crushing a tablet between two spoons.

If you simply cannot administer a tablet or capsule to your cat, check with your veterinarian whether the medication comes in a liquid or paste form. A compounding pharmacist may also be able to reformulate the medication into a liquid or paste form. Another option is to crush the tablet in a pill crusher or between two spoons, dissolve it in 2–5ml of water and administer this suspension to your cat orally via a syringe. Check with your veterinarian whether this is appropriate for your cat's medication. Similarly you may also be able to empty the contents of a capsule out onto your cat's food or dissolve it in water.

Recognising Serious Emergencies

Owners often find it very hard to know whether their cat is having an emergency. They are often faced with the dilemma of whether they should seek veterinary attention or not. You may be left wondering whether the problem can wait until the morning, until Monday or after a public holiday. Cats are like young children in that they cannot tell us that that they are unwell, instead we have to rely on how they behave to let us know. As a result cats can be very sick by the time we realise that they have a problem. In addition animals will attempt to hide their illness and pain as a preservation reflex. Cats are especially good at this and may not show any obvious signs of illness until their condition is very advanced. You know your cat better than anyone else, so in general, if you are worried about your cat it indicates that you should seek veterinary attention. It is far better to see or speak to a veterinarian and have the peace of mind rather than continue to worry and potentially have your cat's condition deteriorate.

This chapter provides a guide to which circumstances are more likely to indicate a serious emergency.

Bleeding

Excessive bleeding, regardless of the cause constitutes an emergency. This may be a result of a traumatic injury and is especially a problem if it is spurting or cannot be stopped by applying direct pressure. Bleeding can also occur in the gut and be present in vomit or stools. Black stools can also indicate bleeding into the gut, although normal cats can have very dark faeces. Blood may discolour the urine indicating a bleeding problem or another lower urinary tract problem. Some mouth ulcers can cause excessive bleeding. Cats may cough blood or they may start bleeding from the nose. A problem with blood clotting can cause bleeding in any part of the body.

Trauma

Any severe trauma such as a road traffic accident, dog attack or a fall from a great height (also known as High-Rise Syndrome) warrants veterinary attention even if the cat involved appears normal (see Trauma on page 46). This is because some injuries may be internal or hidden by fur. Some injuries will not become obvious until some time after the trauma. Cat bites can lead to infections some time after the original injury. It is especially important to seek immediate veterinary attention if the trauma causes obvious bleeding, severe injuries such as broken bones or exposed internal organs, difficulty breathing, paralysis, pain or altered consciousness.

Difficulty breathing

Difficult or laboured breathing at rest is always an emergency. It is important to realise that once a cat shows evidence of difficulty breathing, the problem is severe. There are many causes of breathing difficulty and it is often hard to determine what is causing the problem. Cats with difficulty breathing are often very distressed which exacerbates the problem. Keep your cat as calm as possible, out of the heat and it them to a veterinarian as soon as you can.

Vomiting and diarrhoea

Vomiting and diarrhoea can be emergency situations but they are not always. Cats have a very strong vomiting reflex because as carnivores in the wild they would have to vomit feathers and fur that could potentially cause a life threatening bowel obstruction. Because of this, cats often vomit when there is only a minor upset. Vomiting and diarrhoea are more likely to indicate an emergency if they are severe, rapidly progressive or continue for longer than 24–36 hours. Continued vomiting or diarrhoea will eventually lead to dehydration and so will require veterinary intervention. If the vomit or diarrhoea is large in volume or is very frequent, dehydration is more likely to occur. Vomiting is more likely to lead to dehydration if your cat cannot even hold down water (see Vomiting and Diarrhoea on page 62).

If your cat becomes depressed and generally sick accompanying vomiting or diarrhoea, this indicates that the problem is an emergency. Similarly if your cat also has a fever it indicates a more serious problem. Abdominal pain indicates that the problem is more likely to be an emergency. Signs of pain include yowling, a tense abdomen or hunching in the hind limbs and arching the lower back. Often when cats are in pain they will be very quiet and reclusive, and will curl up rather than stretch out. Your cat may show signs of pain if you try to touch its belly or pick it up.

If your cat's vomit contains fresh blood or digested blood, which looks like coffee grounds and indicates gut bleeding, this is more likely to be an emergency situation. Similarly black or bloody faeces also suggests bleeding into the gut and this is more likely to indicate a serious problem.

If your cat is vomiting and you suspect it has ingested some foreign material such as wool, string or ribbon, it may have a bowel obstruction. If this is the cause of the problem, the vomiting is more likely to be projectile in nature. Your cat may also vomit the string or it may exit its anus. Do not pull on it as this can cause internal damage. A bowel obstruction is a serious emergency situation and you should take your cat to your veterinarian.

If you are concerned that your cat's vomiting and diarrhoea has become complicated by any of the conditions described in this section you should take it to see your veterinarian. You should also take your cat to your veterinarian if it is vomiting or has diarrhoea and is young (less than one year) or elderly (older than eight years) or if it has another medical condition.

Weakness, collapse and paralysis

There are many causes of weakness and collapse; however, whenever this occurs it is likely to indicate a serious problem and so veterinary attention should be sought immediately. These conditions can sometimes be episodic so even if your cat appears to have recovered completely, please do not discount this. Such episodes really need to be investigated by your veterinarian. Severe lethargy, depression or unconsciousness are also emergencies.

There are many causes of paralysis including tick paralysis, (These will be discussed later n the book.) snakebites, spinal problems, nerve diseases and blood clots. Regardless of the cause paralysis is always serious and timely treatment is essential. If you suspect a spinal problem you should use a board to transport your cat, as described on page 55.

Fits

Like humans, cats can have fits, convulsions or seizures although they are not common. They can occur for many reasons. Fits may be as mild as episodes of staring into space or twitching of facial muscles. However, often they are much more dramatic than this and can involve unconsciousness, repeated violent limb movements, frothing at the mouth and often urination and defecation.

Fits or convulsions in cats usually indicate a severe underlying problem. A fit or seizure in itself is of minimal harm as long as it does not go on for greater than 90 seconds. Seizures become very dangerous if they go on much longer than this or if they occur one after the other (see Convulsions, Fits and Seizures on page 72). In any of these cases veterinary assistance should be sought immediately. Be aware that cats can harm themselves during a seizure. If your cat has just had its first mild seizure then it is important to see a veterinarian as soon as possible to try to find out why it happened. If your cat has already been diagnosed with a seizure disorder then a single short seizure may not be a reason to rush it to a veterinarian.

Poisoning
If you know that your cat has ingested a poisonous substance or potentially had exposure to one then this is definitely a reason to seek veterinary assistance. Early intervention can make a huge difference (see Poisoning on page 74 for more information regarding specific poisons). Likewise if you suspect that your cat has been bitten by a snake or poisonous spider you should take it to see your veterinarian.

Allergic reactions
Acute allergic reactions can produce adverse reactions in cats including facial swelling, vomiting and collapse. They can also cause difficulty breathing. If these signs are severe or rapidly progressive you should take your cat to a veterinarian.

Urinary blockage
Inability to urinate can also indicate a serious problem and is a medical emergency. Inability to urinate may indicate a blockage to the urethra and is much more likely to occur in male cats. Your cat may try to urinate without producing anything, or only a few drops, perhaps contaminated with blood. It may strain or even cry out when trying to urinate. Initially your cat may try unsuccessfully to urinate frequently, but as it becomes sicker it may start to

give up trying to urinate all together. Often cats with urinary blockages will lick their genitals excessively, which may make them red and inflamed. If the urinary blockage continues, toxins cannot be excreted and will build up. The bladder can become stretched and damaged or even burst. You should not try to feel for the bladder as it may be very tight, painful and easily burst. If you suspect that your cat has a urinary blockage you should take it to your veterinarian immediately. If you need to carry your cat, lift it from behind its legs rather than under its belly so you do not place pressure on the bladder.

Hyperthermia, fever and hypothermia

Many factors can influence your cat's temperature. However, if it is greater than 39.5°C this may indicate a fever. If this is the case a veterinarian should evaluate your cat. Do not administer anything to your cat to try to alleviate the fever as any such medications have the potential to cause significant harm and may make it harder for your veterinarian to find out why your cat is unwell. If your cat's temperature is less than 37°C it is hypothermic and this may be an emergency (see Hypothermia on page 67).

Eye problems

The eyes are very delicate and precious. Any problem with your cat's eyes is potentially an emergency and time is of the essence. Problems with the eyes can be indicated by a sudden change in their appearance such as swelling, redness, cloudiness, a blue tinge or filling with blood. Excessive discharge can also indicate a problem. An eye problem may be painful and you may notice excessive blinking or holding the eyelids shut. It is especially important to see a veterinarian if the eye has become painful subsequent to trauma such as a fight with another cat. Damaging poisons can enter cats' eyes through accidents or through stink bug (also known as bronze orange, shield, green shield or green vegetable bugs) sprays. If an irritating poison has entered your cat's eyes it should be flushed out thoroughly with water or saline. You should also contact a poisons information service and take your cat to your veterinarian as soon as possible.

Sudden blindness and dilated pupils may indicate high blood pressure causing damage to or detachment of the retinas (the light sensors at the back of the eyes) and is an emergency. Timely treatment is vital with eye problems to avoid long-term problems like blindness (see Eye Problems on page 96).

Kittens and elderly cats

Like babies, kittens are much more fragile than mature cats. Whenever kittens get sick there is always the potential for them to deteriorate very quickly. So if your kitten is unwell you should take them to see your veterinarian as soon as possible. Similarly elderly animals (older than ten years) and animals with other medical issues such as diabetes can become very sick very quickly.

Preventing Emergencies

Unfortunately a lot of emergencies will be completely beyond your control and will occur regardless of what you do. However, there are many things that you can do to help prevent emergencies involving your cat.

Diet

There is great controversy about what is the best diet to feed cats. It is generally accepted that cats are true or obligate carnivores. This means that they require a constant source of animal protein. Most vegetarian diets are not complete and I feel it is unfair to feed a carnivorous animal a vegetarian diet. Cats require a relatively high fat content in their diet as long as they are not overweight. Cats also have a high requirement for various micro-nutrients including thiamin (vitamin B1), niacin (vitamin B3), taurine, arginine, methionine, cystine (essential amino acids) and essential fatty acids. Most high quality commercial diets have ample quantities of these and so commercial cat food should be included in at least part of your cat's diet.

Some raw fish contains enzymes that destroy thiamin and can make a diet thiamine deficient. This is especially true of very strong smelling fish. Similarly some meat for animal consumption contains sulphur preservatives (preservative numbers 220–227) that destroy thiamine normally present in these foods and can lead to thiamine deficiency, which can be very serious (see Reduced Appetite and Anorexia on page 61).

As a general rule, most home-prepared diets are incomplete and will not meet all of a cat's nutritional requirements. At least part of a cat's diet should include a balanced commercial cat food. Dog food is an inadequate diet for a cat.

The most common of these preservatives is sulphur dioxide (220). Mixing these products with other foods will destroy the thiamine in those foods. Cooking foods will also destroy the thiamine in them. Thiamine deficiency is rare as long as at least some component of the diet is a balanced commercial cat food.

Generally as long as raw fish or sulphur-preserved meat is not the only thing you feed your cat, thiamine deficiency is unlikely to develop. Sometimes if a cat stops eating for a period it can become thiamine deficient and this is more likely to occur if its regular diet has been low in thiamine.

Cats with a taurine deficient diet can suffer a heart disease called dilated cardiomyopathy (see Heart Disease on page 101) and degeneration of the retinas (the light sensors at the back of the eyes), which can lead to blindness. As with thiamine deficiency, taurine deficiency is rare in cats that receive at least some balanced commercial cat food in their diet.

As cats are obligate carnivores, they have a low requirement for carbohydrate and some people feel that excessive carbohydrate in a cat's diet may predispose it to obesity and diabetes later in life (see Diabetes on page 96). Possibly because of this low carbohydrate requirement, cats do not have a strong sense of taste for sweet foods so are not adapted for identifying sugars in their diet. Perhaps the easiest way to feed a lower carbohydrate, higher protein diet is to feed a commercial canned food. Dry food generally has higher levels of carbohydrate. Most commercial canned kitten food is very similar to a cat's natural diet.

Environment

While some cats are kept exclusively indoors, others have limited or extensive access to the outdoors. There is a large movement to restrict cats from living outdoors because of their predatory effect on wildlife. There is conflicting evidence and strong opinion regarding this issue and it is not the purpose of this book to give an opinion on this. Some cats do not cope well with being restricted to the indoors. This is especially so if they have become accustomed to having access outdoors. There are some diseases that occur with a higher incidence in cats kept indoors, such as Feline Lower Urinary Tract Disease (see Lower Urinary Problems on page 69) and obesity. However, overall there are probably more hazards to cats kept outdoors and these cats may live shorter lives. Specific hazards include road traffic accidents, catfights and dog attacks (see Trauma on page 46), exposure to various infectious diseases, skin cancer due to sun exposure and even malicious poisoning and injury caused by people who do not like cats.

Of course, hazards also exist indoors, including poisoning (see Poisoning on page 74), ingesting foreign material such as string (see Vomiting and Diarrhoea on page 63), electrocution due to chewing on power cords, and respiratory disease due to exposure to cigarette smoke and other allergens. Cats are very curious animals and will also sometimes get into a washing machine, especially front loaders, or a clothes dryer that is full of clothes or is warm. This can have devastating effects if the cat is not removed before starting a cycle. Cats can quickly burn to death or drown in an operating clothes dryer or washing machine.

Similarly, if you have kittens around you should always keep toilet seats down. Curious kittens can fall into toilet bowls and are often unable to get out their slippery sides.

Always check washing machines or clothes dryers before starting a cycle; cats love these places.

Living indoors in high-rise apartments can also place your cat at risk of High-Rise Syndrome where curious cats fall off high-rise balconies or out of windows and can be seriously injured or even die. This is not uncommon. Often it is impractical to keep your cat completely restricted from these areas. One solution is to build enclosures on decks and balconies so that your cat can safely venture outside. There are companies that manufacture such enclosures.

If a cat lives indoors it should have free access to at least one clean litter tray. The tray should be located in a quiet, private position away from its feeding bowl. It should ideally be in a low traffic area and away from any dogs. There are various litter types available and some enclosed are enclosed to provide more privacy. The main thing is that you provide a litter that your cat likes and that you clean it regularly.

Cats that have pink unpigmented noses, ears and eyelids and live outside are at risk of developing sun damage to these areas of skin. This can lead to the development of skin cancer in these unpigmented areas. This is usually a cancer called squamous cell carcinoma. Ideally such cats should be kept indoors to avoid sun exposure. If you have a cat with unpigmented facial features and it develops any sores, scabs or other lesions on these areas you should take it to your veterinarian.

Cats are very sensitive to stress and this can contribute to and exacerbate various diseases. The biggest cause of stress to a cat is change to its environment. Cats can become very stressed if they move house and it may take two or more weeks for them to become accustomed to a new home. Similarly the arrival of new people or animals in the household or even neighbourhood or the departure of a family member can be very stressful for a cat. It is important that any such change is made as slowly as possible. There are feline pheromone products available that can help reduce stress. These are available as a spray for surfaces or as a plug-in diffuser and are available from your veterinarian. Some cats may benefit from anti-anxiety or anti-depressant medication during times of change and stress or even long-term and you should discuss this with your veterinarian.

It is not uncommon for people to keep cats on boats. Unfortunately, it is also not uncommon for such cats to fall overboard. With no way of climbing back on board the cat can drown. A simple way to reduce the chance of this while you are moored or anchored is to hang a length of carpet over the side of the boat down to the water level. You should try to make your cat aware of the presence of this carpet so that if it does fall overboard it can climb up the carpet and return to safety.

If your cat has access outdoors it can be useful to know roughly where it goes, if anyone else feeds it and if there are any other cats which it come into contact with, and potentially fight with.

What *not to do* when caring for cats

- Do not give your cat paracetamol because it is highly toxic to cats (see Poisoning on page 74). Similarly cats are also sensitive to aspirin, other non-steroidal anti-inflammatory drugs (NSAIDs) and many other prescription medications so you should not administer them unless under the direct instruction of a veterinarian.
- Do not give your cat plain liquid paraffin or mineral oil for any condition, including hair balls or constipation. Cats' throats cannot handle this substance well and there is a risk that the liquid can be aspirated, which can cause severe pneumonia.
- Do not apply any flea or tick products on cats that are labelled for use in dogs only. Some products, especially those that contain permethrin, are often highly toxic to cats (see Synthetic Pyrethroids— Permethrin, under Poisoning on page 82).

- Do not keep lilies in your garden or house if you keep cats. They are highly toxic and cats will readily eat parts of them (see under Poisoning on page 77).

- Do not allow your cat access to automotive radiator coolant or antifreeze. This contains ethylene glycol, which is highly toxic (see under Poisoning on page 78).

- Do not allow your cat access to disinfectant cleaners which contain benzalkalonium chloride. Cats readily ingest these products but they are highly irritating to their mouths and throats (see under Poisoning on page 83).

- Do not let your cat play with string or ribbons. If ingested they can cause serous gastrointestinal damage and blockages (see Vomiting and Diarrhoea on page 63).

- Do not pull on your cat's tail or let children pull on it. This can damage nerves important for urination, defecation, urinary and faecal continence and tail function. Tail pull injuries can be very serious (see Trauma on page 56).

- Do not use collars that are loose enough for your cat to get one of its forelimbs caught in it. The collar may get caught in one of the cat's armpits. This is particularly dangerous if your cat goes missing for a period while this is occurring, as it may result in severe wounds under the arm that will not heal and usually require surgery. There are now collars available that have special clasps that release under tension to prevent this from happening.

Assessing the Feline Emergency Patient

When a person is in an emergency, the most common course of action is for bystanders to administer first aid to them while they wait for an ambulance service to arrive. One reason for this is so that moving the person is left to the professionals thus avoiding further injury. Professional care is then available on the way to a hospital. Unfortunately there is no organised animal ambulance service. Only rarely will a veterinarian be able to attend the scene or provide transport. This means that in most cases cat owners or bystanders have to provide both first aid and transport for the patient. The emphasis therefore, should then be on transporting the patient as quickly and carefully as possible to a veterinary hospital where there are the proper facilities. When assessing the feline emergency patient you should consider: Danger, Response, Airway, Breathing and Circulation (DRABC).

Once you have addressed these things you can worry about the animal's other injuries.

The acronym DRABC can help you remember the most important things to check and what to do for a collapsed patient.

Danger

When dealing with a feline emergency your first priority should be to identify danger to yourself, other people, and then the injured cat. You can potentially become seriously injured trying to assist a cat. If this happens, it further complicates the situation and does not help the patient at all. Often the source of the cat's injury remains a danger to it and others. The patient can also be a danger to you or other people on the scene.

Hit by a car

A cat that has been hit by a car is at risk of being hit again and so are the people trying to help it. This is especially dangerous at night or in bad weather when vision is impaired. It is important to approach the cat when there is a break in traffic. You could also send someone up the street to try to stop oncoming traffic. Your first priority must be to move the cat off the road as carefully as possible to get yourself and the cat out of danger. If you suspect a spinal injury it is important to minimise moving its neck or spine. Ideally the cat should be moved on a board (see Trauma on page 56).

Dog attack

A dog or dogs that are attacking a cat are a serious danger to those trying to stop the attack as well as any bystanders. Any attempt to separate them can be very dangerous and you do so at your own risk. You should avoid placing any of your body parts between the attacking dog and the cat as you may be bitten. There are some techniques that may help separate a dog that is firmly biting down on its victim.

Probably the safest method is to distract the dog, using your voice or by wetting it with a hose or bucket of water. If it is wearing a lead you can pull on this. Pulling on a collar is probably too dangerous as it puts your hands near its mouth. Another tactic is to attack the dog. This is probably the most dangerous course of action as it is the most likely to cause the dog to turn on you. If you do chose this method using makeshift weapons or kicking with an outstretched leg is probably the least dangerous option (remember not to be too brutal even if it has your beloved feline in its grasp).

If the dog is not castrated, grabbing and pulling on its scrotum may cause them to let go.

Electrocution and fires

If the cat you are trying to help has been electrocuted it is vital that you too do not become electrocuted as there may still be live wires around, perhaps that the patient has chewed through.

Before approaching the animal you should turn off the power and unplug any cords if possible. If this is not possible you should use a long wooden pole such as a wooden broom stick to move any live wires away from the patient before approaching it.

Similarly you should not risk becoming trapped in a fire while trying to help a feline emergency patient. You should move yourself and the patient away from a fire and out of danger before administering first aid.

Approaching sick or injured cats

Sick or injured cats are often very scared and in pain. This can make even the most friendly and trusted pet aggressive and a danger to the person attending to it. Cats can be very quick and effective attackers and can cause significant injury. It is very important to be careful not to get bitten or scratched when you are trying to help them.

Approach the cat very slowly and avoid any sudden movements. Watch its body language and look for warning signs:

- ears pinned down flat
- growling, hissing and exposing Its teeth
- erect hairs along back and tail
- raised forelimb, possibly with exposed claws.

Examples of an aggressive cat.

Take notice of these signs and stop approaching a cat that is potentially aggressive. Be aware that cats, especially injured or scared cats can initially be tolerant but very quickly lose their temper and can become aggressive.

Cat bites and scratches can cause serious infections. If you have been bitten or scratched by a cat, you should see your health care professional.

If the cat is relatively receptive or simply too sick or injured to be aggressive, calmly introduce yourself by offering the back of your hand for it to smell. Do not approach the cat from above or behind as it may feel threatened. Make sure that the cat can see you before you touch it. Talk to them quietly and calmly, ideally using its name. If you do not know the cat you may be able to get its name from a tag on its collar.

Squatting next to the cat can make you seem less threatening than if you are standing over it. However, you should not sit down next to them as you may not be able to move away quickly enough if it becomes aggressive.

Often cats are in too much pain for you to do anything to help them or even appreciate the extent of their injuries. Instead you should pick the cat up carefully in order not to hurt it and to avoid being bitten or scratched yourself, then transport it to a veterinarian. If you suspect hind limb injury you should hold it around its belly rather than its hind limbs. If you suspect a spinal injury you should transport the cat on a board as described in Trauma on page 55.

Sometimes throwing a sheet, blanket or towel over a cat that is being aggressive due to pain or fear can help you pick it up more safely and may also help calm the cat. You can also wrap the cat in the blanket to help reduce contamination of its wounds and to protect your car and clothes from blood. Using gardening gloves may help protect your hands.

Responsiveness

Once you have ensured that there is no further danger to yourself, other people or the cat, you should then assess the collapsed cat's response and level of consciousness. Try to rouse the cat to see if it is at all responsive and use its name if you know it. If it does not respond to voices and its name, you can try pinching its toes.

If the cat responds to you it probably does not require resuscitation at that point and you should assess it for shock, difficulty breathing, bleeding and injuries. Such cats may be in a very fragile condition and could deteriorate and stop breathing or their heart could stop. You should continue to monitor their condition closely and take them to a veterinary clinic as soon as possible.

Airway

If a collapsed cat is non-responsive, the first thing you should ensure is that it has an unobstructed airway. Make sure that its head is in a natural or slightly extended position and not bent down towards its chest. Gently pull its tongue forward (take care to avoid being bitten) to help ensure an open airway. You should then check its mouth for foreign objects or fluids such as

saliva, vomit or blood that may be causing an obstruction. You can use your index and middle fingers in a sweeping action at the back of its mouth to clear an obstruction.

A cloth may also be useful to mop up any fluids. If there is a large amount of fluid in the mouth you can elevate the hind quarters so that it drains out. Even holding a cat

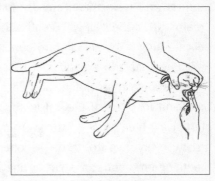

Clearing a collapsed cat's airway.

up by its back legs for 5–10 seconds may help clear fluid from its airway. This can be useful if the patient has suffered near-drowning and has water in its lungs.

Near-drowning sometimes occurs when an animal has fallen into a pool or body of water, perhaps because it has reduced vision, has had a seizure, fallen off the side of a boat or been trapped in a washing machine and a cycle is started.

Do not try to clear the airways of a conscious or a fitting cat as you may be bitten.

Breathing

Once you have cleared the airway, the next step is to check if the cat is breathing. The best way to do this is to put your head next to its head and look at its chest to see if it is rising and falling. This should only take a second or two. If there is no chest movement or if the movements are only very, very small you will need to breathe for the cat. This is best done by mouth-to-nose breathing. You should close the cat's mouth with one hand and cover the cat's nose with your mouth. Then give two slow, long and GENTLE breaths (1–2 seconds each). Between each breath you should watch the chest fall as the air is exhaled. Cats are much smaller than us and have much smaller lungs so they require only very small breaths to fill their lungs. Breaths that are too large risk damaging their delicate lungs. You should only continue the breath until you can see the cat's chest start to expand.

You should then watch the chest again to see if the cat has started breathing for itself. If the cat is still not breathing then you should then start giving breaths at a rate of around 20–30 breaths per minute or one breath every two to three seconds. Do not attempt mouth-to-nose breathing on a conscious cat or one that is breathing for itself.

If your cat has stopped breathing, you may be able to stimulate spontaneous breathing by stimulating an acupuncture point known as Jen Chung or GY 26. This is located on the nose. To stimulate GY 26 you should insert a needle (ideally sterile) several millimetres into this point and move it around while continuing to monitor for improvements in your cat's breathing (see picture on next page). If you do not have a needle you can firmly pinch this region.

If your cat is having ANY difficulty breathing you should take it to a veterinarian immediately.

Circulation

The next step is to check the cat's circulation. This means checking if the cat has a heartbeat or a pulse. These can be checked by feeling the heartbeat on the chest wall or feeling for a femoral pulse. You should also check its gum colour (see Being Prepared on page 12). This information can give you some

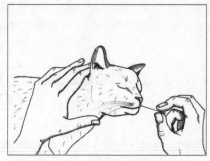

A needle being inserted in GY 26.

idea of whether the animal is suffering shock. In the early stages of shock patients will have elevated heart and pulse rates (greater than 180–200 beats per minute). The pulse may feel normal or bounding. The gums will remain a normal pink colour. As shock progresses the pulse will become weaker and the gums may become pale. The cat's temperature may also fall and its limbs and ears may feel cool. When shock becomes very advanced, the pulse will be weak, the gums will be pale, the body temperature will be reduced and the heart and pulse rates will have dropped (less than 120 beats per minute). Once shock is this advanced it is very serious and the cat's heart may stop at any time. You should be prepared to start Cardiopulmonary Resuscitation or CPR as described in the next chapter. Note that pain may produce signs very similar to early shock. Shock due to infection may cause elevated heart and pulse rates with brick red gums and an elevated body temperature.

If the cat you are assessing has a heartbeat you should continue to breathe for the cat until it starts to breathe on its own again. Continuously monitor its heartbeat or pulses during mouth-to-nose breathing. If there is no pulse or heartbeat, or it stops while you are performing mouth-to-nose breathing you will need to start CPR as is described in the next chapter.

Once you have assessed the patient you should assess the scene itself. There may be vomit or diarrhoea at the scene. There may be evidence of a toxin that the cat has eaten. If a snakebite was the cause there may be an injured or dead snake in the area. If the cat has been electrocuted there may be evidence of chewed power cords in the area. If the cat has suffered trauma it may have frayed claws (see Trauma on page 46).

Cardiopulmonary Resuscitation (CPR)

The major difference between CPR in humans and cats is that the purpose of CPR in humans is to try to keep the patient alive until ambulance staff can attend. They then continue resuscitation and transport the person to a hospital. As there is no specialised ambulance service for cats, your major aim is to transport your cat to a veterinary hospital as soon as possible while using CPR to keep it alive in the meantime. A veterinary hospital can provide much more assistance than you can give in a first aid situation. Also, cats that require CPR often do need it repeatedly so there is no point spending valuable time trying to fully resuscitate the cat at the scene only to have it stop breathing or have its heart stop beating again when you are no closer to a veterinary clinic and specialised care. Limited resuscitation can continue in the car on the way to the veterinary clinic.

A cat can stop breathing and its heart can stop beating for numerous reasons. It can occur suddenly for example after it has suffered serious trauma or electrocution. It can also occur as a result of gradual deterioration of a cat's condition due to another disease. Once you have assessed a collapsed patient and determined that it is non-responsive, is not breathing for itself and does not have a heartbeat or pulse as described in the previous chapter, you should start CPR.

If the patient is not breathing on its own you should be giving it mouth-to-nose breathing at approximately 20–30 breaths per minute as described in Assessing the Feline Emergency Patient on page 40. Once you have checked the circulation, if there is no heartbeat or pulse you need to start chest compressions.

There are many different techniques for performing chest compressions. You will have to adjust the technique you use based on how effective you are being in creating a detectable pulse and improving gum colour. The cat should be lying on its side and you should apply firm compressions directly over the heart, which is located in the chest roughly in line with the elbow. The compressions should be firm enough to depress the chest wall around 2 centimetres. You should do this at a rate of 120 compressions per minute or two compressions every second. To apply the chest compressions use the palm of one had over the heart with the other had either under the cat's chest or supporting the cat's body. If you have large hands you can also use your thumb to apply cardiac compressions (see the illustrations which show several different techniques).

When you perform chest compressions it is possible to break ribs or bruise the lungs, this is not the end of the world if it happens but is preferably avoided. There is a fine balance between being effective and doing damage.

If you are performing CPR with two people, you should aim to give one breath every 4–6 chest compressions. This breath should be given between compressions and you should ideally do this without a pause in the compressions. The second operator can check how effective you are being by feeling for a femoral pulse. If there is no pulse you can change your technique slightly. You can increase or decrease the compression rate or you could increase or decrease the compression force. You can also look to see if the gum colour is improving. If you have a third person helping they can apply continuous firm pressure to the belly with their hands as this can also increase effectiveness.

If you are performing the CPR alone, you should give two long

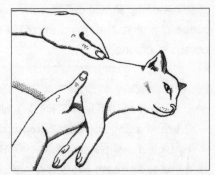

Cat receiving CPR: thumb applying compressions.

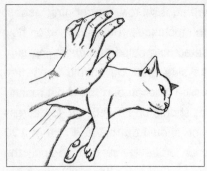

Cat receiving CPR: hand on hand

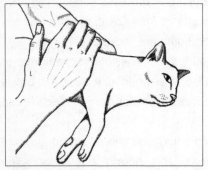

Cat receiving CPR: hand on back.

gentle breaths every 15 compressions. You will obviously have to have a pause in the compressions to do this.

You should check to see if the cat's heart has started beating on its own by briefly stopping the chest compressions and feeling for a heartbeat or pulse once every minute. If there is no heartbeat or pulse you will have to keep going. If there is a heartbeat or the pulse has returned, continue to monitor this while giving mouth-to-nose breathing at 20–30 breaths per minute until the cat starts breathing for itself again.

Some people believe that chest compressions alone help move enough air in and out of the lungs. This means that during CPR, if the heart has stopped beating your priority should be chest compressions rather than breathing. If you are having trouble coordinating them both, the mouth-to-nose breathing should definitely be discontinued first. This is especially true during the first five minutes of CPR, after which time breathing also becomes important.

One person feline CPR: 120 chest compressions per minute, 2 breaths per 15 chest compressions.
Two or more person feline CPR: 120 chest compressions per minute, 1 breath every 4–6 chest compressions.

During CPR large amounts of air may build up in the stomach causing it to become very swollen. If this is occurring you can take a few seconds to push on the stomach to try to relieve this when it is needed.

Do not attempt to perform chest compressions on a cat with a heartbeat or a pulse.

A cat can stop breathing and its heart can stop beating for many reasons. To some degree, the actual cause determines the chance of resuscitation efforts being successful. Unfortunately once a cat has stopped breathing, especially if its heart has stopped, there is only a small chance that it will ultimately survive. As stated above, this chance is increased by getting it to a veterinary hospital as soon as possible. There is also the chance that if it does recover it will have temporary or permanent neurological problems. However, even a small chance of success makes it very worthwhile for those who survive so resuscitation should be attempted. If a heartbeat has not been restored after 20 minutes of resuscitation, there is very little chance that the cat will survive the ordeal. If it does survive it is very likely to have severe neurological problems so you should consider discontinuing all efforts after this period.

Trauma

There are many ways your cat can get hurt. Common ways are being hit by a car, catfights causing bites and scratches, dog attacks, becoming caught in fences or traps and so-called High-Rise Syndrome. Occasionally cats will become victims of animal abuse. These incidents can cause both external injuries, including: bruising, grazes and lacerations and internal injuries of varying severity. Sometimes trauma can cause significant bleeding which in itself can be life threatening, as well as bone fractures, dislocations and even spinal injuries. Cats also suffer burns just as we do. Sometimes itchy cats will damage themselves when they scratch excessively.

Often cats who have suffered major trauma such as being hit by a car will try to run away. This does not mean that they are not hurt and you should not discount their injuries. They are very scared and confused and are instinctively trying to get away from danger. They may still have life threatening injuries. Sometimes cats return home after receiving significant trauma. One common sign of trauma is frayed claws indicating that a cat has instinctively tried to dig into the ground. You can examine your cat's claws by carefully sqeezing its paw to express its claws. If your cat has suffered major trauma, you should take it to your veterinarian as soon as possible.

When you are assessing a victim of major trauma it is important to

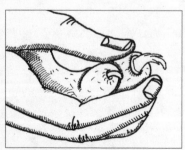

Expressing a cat's frayed claws.

note any difficulty breathing as this may indicate a serious chest injury. Such injuries can get worse very quickly so you should take your cat to your veterinarian immediately.

Major trauma has the potential to damage the urinary bladder or other parts of the urinary system. It is important to note if your cat has urinated after a traumatic injury, also note if the urine is bloody. This is very important information to provide to your veterinarian. The presence of blood in the faeces is also potentially significant. Other internal organs may be damaged in major trauma. Often these injuries are not outwardly apparent for 36–72 hours after the initial injury.

Bleeding

Many different types of injuries can cause bleeding. A graze can cause a small amount of oozing of blood due to capillary damage. Damage to veins can cause blood to trickle out. The most serious type of bleeding is from arteries because this causes the most rapid loss of blood and is the hardest to stop. Bleeding from arteries will cause blood to spurt out in pulses. Bleeding that occurs on the outside of the cat's body is usually quite easy to detect. If you detect large amounts of bleeding, the best way to slow or stop this is to apply pressure to the source of the bleeding. You can use gauze swabs from your feline first aid kit (see page 18), or another piece of cloth such as clothing or a towel to apply firm pressure to the source of bleeding. If the gauze cloth becomes soaked in blood do not remove it as this may disturb any blood clots, instead use more gauze or cloth on top of this. Hold this pressure until you can transfer your cat into your veterinarian's care or the bleeding stops.

If direct pressure is not controlling the bleeding and it is continuing to spurt from an arterial source, you can also try holding above the wound firmly to try and hold off the supplying artery. If capillary or venous bleeding is continuing to ooze or trickle out, you can also try holding just below the wound firmly to try to stop venous blood flow to the wound. These techniques are useful if the bleeding is coming from a limb or the tail. Continue to apply direct pressure to the bleeding while doing this.

If this is still not controlling the bleeding from a limb or the tail, you can also try elevating the source of the bleeding above the level of the heart.

Bleeding can also be internal. It can occur into the chest or into the abdomen and can be very difficult to detect and sometimes is very slow.

Bleeding into the chest may cause difficulty breathing. This may or may not be evident initially instead manifesting over the 24–36 hours following trauma. Cats that have bled into their chest may cough up blood. Bleeding into the abdomen may cause some abdominal distension but only if it is severe. It may also cause abdominal pain. Cats that are bleeding may be in shock (see Assessing the Feline Emergency Patient on page 41). There is nothing that you can do about internal bleeding so if there is any doubt you should rush your cat to your veterinarian immediately.

Excessive bleeding from the mouth can be due to excessive grooming over a long period wearing down the roof of the mouth. This can cause a so-called indolent or rodent ulcer over one of the arteries on the roof of the mouth. This can cause very serious bleeding and if you suspect such an ulcer you should take your cat straight to a veterinarian.

Skin tears and lacerations

The most common injury received from trauma is damage to the skin and underlying tissue. There may be large tears due to bite wounds, or where a limb has become caught in a fence or come in contact with a car or the ground. Road traffic accidents may also cause severe grazes where the skin has come into contact with the road. Sharp edges of fractured bones may cause wounds where they penetrate the skin. Sharp objects can also cut the skin, especially in the pads. Sometimes wounds are much more extensive than they appear externally. With all wounds it is important to minimise further contamination before the cat can be seen by a veterinarian. You should try to stop your cat from licking the wounds. If you have been given an Elizabethan collar (also known as a bucket collar)

Cat wearing an Elizabethan collar.

by your veterinarian for a previous problem you can put this on your cat. These are large plastic collars that project over your cat's head to help prevent it from chewing and licking. Wearing latex examination gloves when handling the wound will also help minimise contamination as well as protect you from contact with the cat's blood.

Any wound can become infected so if there is any delay in seeking veterinary attention you should flush the wound out using saline (preferably sterile) from a syringe. Do not try to flush or clean a wound that is bleeding profusely as this may encourage further bleeding instead attempt to stop the bleeding. To flush skin wounds, simply fill the syringe with saline and squirt it using reasonable pressure into the wound. You can also gently introduce the tip of the syringe under any flaps of skin and squirt saline under these areas. If there are large amounts of contamination to a wound with hair, dirt, grass or bitumen it may be more useful to pour large volumes of saline onto the wound to wash this off before trying to flush the wound out. You can then fill a wound with a sterile water-based lubricant either after you have flushed the wound or while you transport your cat to your veterinarian as a measure to help prevent further contamination. If your cat has long hair, you can carefully cut hair from around the wound to help prevent contamination from it. It is important that this is done after the wound has been filled with a sterile water-based lubricant to help prevent the cut hairs contaminating the wound.

The wound can further be protected by applying a light dressing before you can take your cat to your veterinarian. This can be difficult especially if your cat is in great pain, so only do it if you feel confident and if your cat is not resisting too much. Certain areas on the cat's body can be very difficult to bandage such as the shoulder, hips and thigh. Consequently it is often much better to leave the wound management to your veterinarian.

Bandaging wounds

You can bandage wounds on the limbs, pads or body by first gently placing any flaps of skin back down where they normally sit. Dry the area with swabs

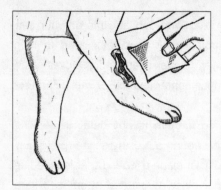

Applying a non-adhesive dressing.

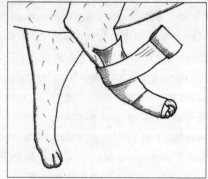

Applying roll-cotton, conforming gauze, then adhesive bandage.

before bandaging the wound. You should then apply a non-adherent dressing over the wound itself. Next, apply a layer of roll-cotton dressing over this. Each turn of the roll-cotton dressing should overlap the previous one by approximately half the width of the bandage. If you are bandaging a limb you should start at the toes and work up. Then apply a layer of conforming gauze over this, again starting at the toes if you are bandaging a limb. This should be firm but not too tight as this can reduce blood supply to the area or interfere with breathing if it is on the body. Again each turn should overlap the previous one by about half the width of the dressing. Finally you can apply the adhesive bandage to help hold this in place. This can be very sticky and difficult to unravel so before placing the bandage you should unravel it completely by either having someone else hold onto one end or stick it onto a table and then re-roll it. Again this is applied over the other layers starting at the toe and overlapping each turn. Be very careful not to make this layer too tight as in general there is a tendency to do so.

You should be able to fit two fingers between the bandage and the body part being bandaged. If you cannot, it is too tight. You should also continue the adhesive layer of the bandage for about 3–4 centimetres beyond the other layers so that it sticks directly to the skin or fur to help hold the bandage on. If you are bandaging the body, sometimes the bandage tends to slip down towards the tail. To try to stop this you should extend the

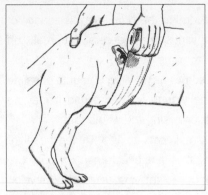

Applying a body bandage.

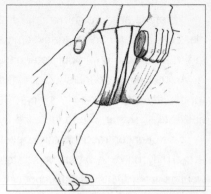

Extend the adhesive bandage 3–4 cm toward the head, overlapping the other layers.

adhesive bandage 3–4 centimetres towards the head beyond the other layers of the bandage.

Ideally any bandage that you have placed should not stay on for more than six hours before the animal is checked by a veterinarian. If it is on longer than two hours you should check the animal's toes every hour to make sure that they have not become swollen or overlapping and that they are still warm. If they are swollen or cold, this means the bandage is cutting off the blood supply to the toes and needs to be removed.

Puncture wounds and embedded foreign objects

Puncture wounds can occur due to injures such as animal bites, especially cat bites, or a sharp object such as a splinter puncturing the skin. Sometimes the offending object remains embedded in the skin. Puncture wounds, particularly those caused by animal bites, are especially at risk of becoming infected.

Animal bites can also cause much more extensive injury than is apparent superficially. Sometimes large amounts of the tissue deep to the skin is involved and the skin may have become detached over a large area although only a small puncture wound may be seen externally. This is often true when a dog picks up and shakes its victim. So all puncture wounds should be examined by your veterinarian.

If there is any foreign material embedded in the skin, such as a piece of glass or a splinter, try to gently remove it with some tweezers. If it breaks off in the skin leave it for your veterinarian to remove.

Any puncture wound should be flushed out using large amounts of saline (preferably sterile) from a syringe. If the wound is on the pad it may be easier to soak the wound in saline by submersing the whole foot.

It is not uncommon for cats, especially male cats, to fight. During a catfight a cat may become bitten or scratched. It is not uncommon for puncture wounds from fights to go unnoticed and catfight abscesses may develop several days after a fight. These are due to infections introduced when a cat is bitten by another cat and subsequent accumulation of pus under the skin. Often the first thing that is noticed is a soft swelling under the skin. The overlying skin may or may not be painful, hot, reddened or bruised. Abscesses can make your cat quite sick causing a fever, reduced appetite and lethargy. Sometimes if a puncture wound is missed or even if it has been treated appropriately there is the potential for it to become infected and for an abscess to form. Commonly abscesses rupture and the first thing that you notice is foul-smelling pus or bloody material oozing out and covering the surrounding hair. Often cats feel much better once the abscess has ruptured. You can use sterile saline to further flush out the ruptured abscess.

Sometimes infections from cat bites can extend into the chest cavity. This can cause pus to accumulate in the space around the lungs (pyothorax or thoracic empyema). This can cause a fever (or hypothermia in its advanced stages), a poor appetite, lethargy, depression and difficulty breathing, especially when your cat breathes in. Like a lot of cat diseases, the signs are often not obvious until the condition is advanced, this is especially true of the difficulty breathing. This is very serious and if you suspect that your cat may have pyothorax you should take it to your veterinarian immediately.

Cats that fight are at increased risk of contracting several different viruses because they can be transmitted through bites. One such virus is Feline Immunodeficiency Virus (FIV), which is a virus similar to Human Immunodeficiency Virus (HIV) although it cannot be passed on to humans.

Another is the Feline Leukaemia Virus (FeLV). Both of these viruses can cause a range of problems but cats can potentially live normally for years after infection. The frequency of infection with these viruses varies from place to place around the world but FIV infection is relatively common in cats in Australia while FeLV infection is quite rare. Vaccinations are now available against both of these viruses but there are several considerations before deciding to have your cat vaccinated. These include your cat's risk of infection, its current infection status and whether your cat is microchipped. You should discuss these issues with your veterinarian.

Broken bones

Cats that are victims of traumatic incidents may suffer broken bones (or fractures) and dislocations. These may be contained within the body or the fractured ends of the bone can be become externalised through the skin. This often makes external fractures easy to identify. Internal fractures can be identified by acute non-weight bearing lameness in the affected limb. The limb may be held in an abnormal

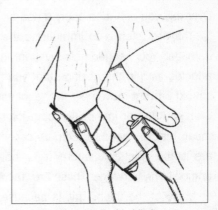

Cat with splinted lower hind limb.

position. There may be obvious instability of the limb at the site of the fracture where it swings unnaturally. Ultimately an X-ray is needed to identify a fracture. Bone injuries are very painful so you should not try to replace externalised fracture ends, realign the limb or manipulate the area in any way. Doing so also has the potential to do further damage.

Cats that have been hit by a car often sustain fractures to the pelvis, which may be initially less obvious and requires veterinary evaluation. Dislocation of the joint between the two lower jaws is another common injury in cats that have been hit by a car or fallen from a great height. If this has occurred your cat may have its mouth open and there may be some asymmetry in the position of the lower canine teeth. There may also be some bleeding in the region.

Bone fractures are very serious and you should take your cat to a veterinarian as soon as possible. You should minimise contamination of any externalised fractures, as bone infections can be very serious. When handling an external fracture you should wear examination gloves.

If there is going to be a delay in seeing a veterinarian, the wound can be flushed with saline (ideally sterile) from a syringe to help remove any hair or dirt. You can then fill the wound with sterile water-based lubricant (ideally from a previously unopened packet) to help prevent further contamination. Over this you can then apply a non-adherent dressing to the wound.

The next step is to immobilise the limb in an attempt to avoid further damage. You can do this by applying an immobilising bandage to the affected limb in the position that you find it. To be effective, your bandage should prevent movement in the joints above and below the fracture.

If you do not immobilise both joints, the movement in those joints will mean that the bandage actually causes more harm than good. Also, there are some fractures where it is not appropriate for you to apply an immobilising bandage. These are fractures of the forelimb above the elbow or those of the thigh. This is because it is very difficult to immobilise the shoulder or hip. So bandaging limbs with fractures at these locations will always be detrimental. In these cases you should take your cat to a veterinarian with no bandaging. You should still try to keep your cat as quiet and as calm as possible and the limb as still as possible. Do not attempt to apply an immobilising bandage if your cat is struggling too much as this also has the potential to cause more harm.

Do not attempt to place immobilising bandages to fractures of the upper forelimb or thigh.

Applying immobilising bandages to fractured limbs is similar to applying bandages to skin wounds on the limbs. The main difference is that you should use much more roll-cotton dressing in the padded layer of the bandage so that it restricts the limb movement and protects the fractured leg. Not using enough cotton wool may cause the bandage to move the fractured bone ends excessively and cause further damage. If you feel confident you can also fashion a makeshift splint. Possibilities include using a piece of wood or thick cardboard, newspaper or a magazine contoured around the limb.

This splint should ideally extend over both joints either side of the fracture. You should attach the splint over the conforming gauze layer using tape around the entire limb at multiple evenly spaced locations. If you do not have tape you can tie it in place using multiple gauze or cloth strips. You can then place the adhesive layer over this.

Spinal injuries

Trauma can cause a spinal injury such as a fractured or dislocated back or neck. Spinal damage should be suspected after all major trauma and trauma patients should all be moved very carefully. Signs of spinal damage include the patient not being able to move or possibly feel its hind limbs or even all of its limbs. Sometimes the forelimbs may be unnaturally stiff and extended. The cat may dribble urine and may have an unusually open anus. The injured cat may or may not be in a lot of pain. Sometimes cats with a spinal injury are surprisingly comfortable given the degree of their injuries because their ability to detect pain has been reduced by the injury. If you are concerned that a feline trauma victim has suffered spinal injury it is best to play it safe and you should minimise moving it. The safest way to transport the cat to a veterinarian is to gently slide a stiff board, usually wooden, under the patient. Ideally someone should hold and support the cat during this to minimise movement, especially its neck and back. You should then use strips of cloth or soft rope tied around the patient and the board to secure it. You can then carefully lift the board and transport the animal to a veterinary hospital.

Tail pull injuries

Cats are very sensitive to having their tail pulled. If your cat's tail is pulled, this can damage the delicate nerve roots in the base of its spine. This can result in reduced tail function, which causes the tail to be carried low, flaccid, and unable to move. Occasionally this means that the tail ultimately needs to be amputated. Tail pull injuries can also make it difficult for cats to urinate and empty their bladder or pass faeces. Tail pull injuries can cause the anus to lose its normal tone and cause faecal incontinence. These deficiencies sometimes improve with time but can be permanent. You should never pull your cat's tail and instruct children not to do so. If you suspect that you cat has suffered a tail pull injury you should take it to your veterinarian.

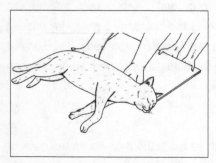

Carefully slide a stiff board under the cat.

Bruises

Bruises are an accumulation of blood under the skin or within tissues. This blood initially causes reddening to the skin and there may be some pain and swelling. This blood gradually breaks down changing colour during this process. Bruises can be caused by blunt trauma. They can also occur due to an underlying problem such as a clotting disorder. If your cat has a bruise and you can identify a

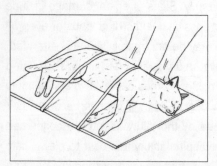

Secure the cat to the board for transport.

sensible reason why it became bruised such as mild blunt trauma, you can treat this with cool compresses. These can be commercial cool packs, ice or frozen vegetables wrapped in a towel. Cool compresses should be applied to the area for 15 minutes four times a day until it has resolved. This may take several days. If you are concerned about the bruise and do not know how your cat has sustained it you should take your cat to your veterinarian.

Burns

Cats can suffer burns in the same way as humans. Often the extent of the burn is masked by the presence of hair over the skin. Burnt skin will be red, swollen and painful. More severe burns will cause the skin to weep, blister and peel. Burns can be thermal due to contact with a hot surface such as a barbeque, a motorbike or a car exhaust pipe, or a hot liquid such as boiling water. They can also be due to contact with damaging chemicals. In an emergency situation, the most important thing that you can do for your cat is to remove it from the source of the burn. Again it is vital not to injure yourself. Once you have done this you should aim to minimise the damage caused. If the burn is due to heat, the treatment is copious amounts of cool running water to cool the area for at least 30 minutes.

> **Regardless of the cause of the burn, it should initially be treated with large amounts of cool running water.**

If the burn has been due to contact with an irritant chemical, this should be thoroughly washed off the skin and hair using cool running water and perhaps mild shampoo or detergent if required. You can use a hose to achieve this; however, the water pressure should not be too high as this can be painful. Using multiple buckets of water is also very effective. Sometimes if your cat is not being cooperative using slightly tepid water may help. Once you have cooled the skin or washed off the chemical you should take your cat to you veterinarian. Take the packaging with you. If the burn has been due to a chemical, you should also call a poisons information service (see Emergency Contacts on page 111).

You should not apply any butter, oils, petroleum jelly or ointments on burns. Instead have them assessed by your veterinarian.

Cats that have been electrocuted often suffer burns where the current has entered its body, often the mouth, and also where it has exited. Once the cat's condition has been stabilised these burns can be treated as described previously. Burns in the mouth region may be difficult to cool with water and cool compresses may be more appropriate.

Bandaging neck.

Note that cats that have suffered electrocution may suffer serious consequences such as fluid build up in the lungs (pulmonary oedema) and difficulty breathing hours after the event. Your cat should be seen by your veterinarian as soon as possible, even if it seems well.

You should keep power cords out of reach of your cat, apply special covers available from electrical and hardware stores which can protect exposed power cords and install safety switches to help guard against electrocution of your cat.

Self-trauma

Sometimes when cats are very itchy they can lick or scratch themselves excessively. This can be due to a variety of skin conditions including allergies, fleas and mites, contact with irritant substances and acute hypersensitivity or allergic reactions. Licking generally only causes damage if it is excessive or continues over a long time. You can apply an Elizabethan collar if you have one. You can also try applying a deterrent substance such as Vicks VapoRub®, Tabasco sauce, or a commercial product like Woundguard® or bitter apple to the area. This will deter some cats from licking; however, most itchy cats are too determined to be distracted by this.

Scratching with the hind limbs has the potential to cause quite serious skin injuries. If your cat is scratching excessively and you fear that it is damaging itself you should take it to your veterinarian. Itchy cats can be quite distressed and you should have the problem investigated and treated as soon as possible. If there will be a delay in seeing a veterinarian, you can bandage their hind paws, covering their claws to help reduce the damage that they can cause. The technique you should use is similar to that used to bandage a limb as described above but it only needs to cover the paw.

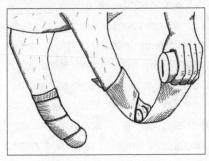

Bandaging the feet of a cat.

First apply a padded layer of roll-cotton dressing, starting at the toes and covering the whole foot. Then continue bandaging upwards almost to the hock. Ensure you have used a reasonable amount of padding over the claws so they are well covered. Then apply conforming gauze over this. Finally apply adhesive bandage over this and continue it around 4 centimetres past the other layers so that it sticks to the fur. Some cats are very good at getting bandages off so you may have to reapply them. Putting a deterrent substance such as Vicks VapoRub®, Tabasco sauce, Woundguard® or bitter apple on the bandages may help stop them chewing them off. If your cat is primarily scratching its neck, you can apply a bandage over this region to help protect it. Be careful not to make it too tight. Trimming the hind claws may also help minimsise the damage that an itchy cat can do to itself.

Reduced Appetite and Anorexia

Cats can have fickle appetites much to the frustration of their owners. A reduced appetite or complete anorexia is a non-specific feature of many feline illnesses. In itself this usually does not help distinguish the problem but simply indicates that the cat is unwell. However, some features of anorexia can help localise the problem. If your cat is interested in food but turns away from it at the last minute or after only a tiny bit, this may indicate pain or difficulty associated with eating or swallowing. This can be caused by dental disease such as loose or broken teeth, gingivitis or periodontitis, which is very common in cats and is indicated by a line of inflammation at the margins of the gums. Certain viruses can cause gingivitis or inflammation of the gums. There are many other causes of a painful mouth and all tend to cause drooling and difficulty or reluctance to eat. Sometimes the problem is a painful food pipe (oesophagus). This may also be accompanied by drooling and excessive swallowing, even when the cat is not eating. Any cause of nausea can also cause cats to initially appear interested in food but then turn away before eating.

Other causes of anorexia can be due to problems with the stomach and intestines. Gastrointestinal problems range from simple gastroenteritis, which in itself has many causes and is usually accompanied by vomiting and diarrhoea. Other possibilities include more serious conditions such as an intestinal obstruction due to an ingested foreign object or even a gastrointestinal cancer.

Anorexia can also be caused by problems outside the gastrointestinal tract, which make the cat feel unwell. There are numerous causes of this including infections such as catfight abscesses (see Trauma on page 52), cat flu, liver conditions, pancreatitis, kidney problems (see Kidney Problems on page 100) and various cancers.

If a cat is anorexic for a prolonged period (greater than 48 hours), it may become dehydrated, especially if it is also not drinking, is vomiting or has diarrhoea. Cats can also get other complications of anorexia including weight loss. Another condition that can develop secondary to anorexia is hepatic lipidosis. In this condition fat stores are mobilised rapidly due to starvation. The liver's systems for metabolising fat become overwhelmed and it becomes infiltrated with fat. This causes the liver function to decline and is a very serious condition in itself that requires aggressive treatment by your veterinarian. Obese cats, especially males, are at increased risk of this condition and should receive attention early if they are anorexic.

Cats have some unique dietary requirements including a high requirement for thiamine. If a cat has not been eating, it may be at risk of developing a thiamine deficiency. Cats that have been fed a marginally thiamine deficient diet prior to becoming anorexic are especially at risk. Signs of thiamine deficiency include depression, weakness, tremors, dilated pupils and curling of the head down towards the forelimbs.

If your cat has a poor appetite or is completely anorexic, you need to try to find out why it is not eating. This often requires your veterinarian to investigate and treat the problem. Things that you can do to encourage your cat to eat include offering it a variety of its favourite foods. Tempting it with warmed or strongly smelling fishy foods including sardines or smoked salmon may help. Hand feeding can be useful. If your cat still will not eat, one option is force feeding. You can use a syringe to carefully administer pureed food. This is not appropriate if your cat is overly weak or collapsed because of the risk of it aspirating the food into its lungs, which can cause pneumonia. It is also not appropriate if your cat is vomiting.

If your cat remains anorexic you should take it to see your veterinarian and have its condition investigated and treated. Various appetite stimulants may also be appropriate if the cause of the anorexia is not readily evident. You should discuss this with your veterinarian.

Vomiting and Diarrhoea

Cats are natural carnivores and in the wild eat most of their prey. For their digestive system to deal with this they often have to vomit to expel feathers, fur and bones. Because of this, domestic cats are good at vomiting and even a mild disturbance can cause vomiting. There are numerous causes of vomiting and diarrhoea. Sometimes the problem can be due to a mild reaction to food or a mild infection and will spontaneously resolve within several days. Alternatively vomiting can indicate very serious conditions such as a gastrointestinal obstruction, liver, kidney or hormonal disorder or even cancer. Similarly diarrhoea can be due to a mild upset or due to a more serious disturbance. Often it is impossible for you to judge whether the vomiting or diarrhoea is something that will resolve by itself or if it indicates a more serious problem. Recognising Serious Emergencies on page 23 gives some guidelines on when these problems are likely to be emergencies.

Hairballs or fur balls can also cause vomiting and are due to excess hair ingestion. This is more likely to occur in long-haired cats but it can also occur in cats with itchy skin conditions including flea infestations which can cause over grooming. Occasionally over grooming can be due to behavioural conditions. Most of the time hairballs can be dislodged by administering a laxative designed for cats. Occasionally hairballs will become solidified in the stomach or intestines and cause persistent vomiting. If this is the case the hairball may need to be removed surgically. If you suspect a hairball is present, it is reasonable to use laxatives designed for cats for 24–48 hours. If your cat continues to vomit or if it becomes anorexic or depressed you should take it to see your veterinarian. You should not use laxatives designed for people. You should NOT administer plain liquid paraffin or mineral oil to your cat. Cats' throats do not handle these substances well and they can aspirate it, which can cause a severe pneumonia. Brushing long-haired cats, applying flea treatments and managing any skin or behavioural condition in conjunction with your veterinarian can help prevent hairballs. Feeding a commercial diet designed to help prevent hairballs may also be beneficial.

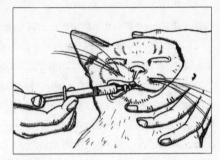

Carefully feeding a cat with a syringe.

Cats love to play with string, sewing thread, wool and ribbon. Sometimes cats will ingest this, which can cause a serious problem because it can cause the intestines to become bunched up on themselves, which can lead to an obstruction. The string can eventually cut through the intestines, causing leakage of intestinal contents into the abdomen. This can be life threatening. Sometimes sewing thread that your cat has ingested will have a needle attached and this can be even more serious. If you suspect that your cat has ingested some string or ribbon, you should take it to your veterinarian, especially if it is vomiting or unwell. If your cat has a string or thread coming out of its mouth or anus you should NOT pull on it as this can cause internal injury. Instead take your cat to your veterinarian as soon as possible. Also do not cut any string that is exiting from your cat's mouth or anus as this can make its removal more difficult for your veterinarian. You should discourage your cat from playing with string, ribbon or thread and keep these items out of your cat's reach.

If you feel that the vomiting or diarrhoea is not or not yet an emergency, the best thing that you can do is to feed your cat a bland food such as lean boiled chicken or a commercial feline gastrointestinal diet available from your veterinarian for 3–7 days. If your cat continues to vomit or have profuse diarrhoea despite being fed only a bland food or if it is not interested in food, you should take it to see your veterinarian. I do not recommend that you fast your cat for prolonged periods, because cats require a constant source of nutrition; they should not be fasted for more than 12–24 hours.

If the problem seems to have resolved, you can then gradually reintroduce your cat's normal diet over the next seven days.

Other treatments for vomiting and diarrhoea should only be used if they are specifically prescribed by your veterinarian.

Vomiting can also cause a problem if your cat is on regular oral medication. This is because when a cat is vomiting you cannot be sure that it is receiving its medication. This may be especially dangerous if your cat has a heart condition. So if your cat is vomiting and has a life-threatening condition requiring long-term oral medication, you should take it to a veterinarian as missing even one dose may be dangerous. Your veterinarian may be able to give the medication or an alternative medication as an injection rather than orally.

Dehydration

Like a poor appetite, dehydration is a common but non-specific sign of disease. Because cats evolved in desert environments they are very good at concentrating their urine and conserving water, also they often do not have a strong thirst drive. Cats get most of their water through their diet rather than drinking. This means that if they stop eating for any reason (see Reduced Appetite and Anorexia on page 60), they can dehydrate quickly. This is compounded if there is vomiting or diarrhoea, which can increase body water and electrolyte loss. Dehydration can be assumed if there has been prolonged anorexia with or without vomiting or diarrhoea. Cats with kidney problems (kidney or renal insufficiency or failure) will continue to produce excessive amounts of urine even if they are not drinking a lot. Similarly cats on diuretic therapy because of heart conditions will continue to produce excessive urine, even if their water intake is reduced. Such cats can quickly become dehydrated if they stop eating and drinking, or have vomiting or diarrhoea.

Sometimes cats return home in a dehydrated state after being away for a period. In this situation there is often no obvious cause for the dehydration. It is possible that your cat has become trapped somewhere without access to food or water, or perhaps has had an illness such as vomiting or diarrhoea that has now resolved but left it in a dehydrated state.

Signs of dehydration include skin tenting. This is when the skin will stay elevated longer than normal when it is pinched up. This can be hard to interpret if your cat has lost a lot of weight or is very thin. Dry or tacky gums can also indicate dehydration. However, moist gums do not completely rule out dehydration because they can become moist if there is excessive salivation due to nausea.

Regardless of the cause of dehydration, it is important for it to be corrected. As long as there is no serious underlying or ongoing illness, sometimes rehydration alone will be enough to make a cat well again. Options for rehydration include offering your cat palatable foods (see Reduced Appetite and Anorexia on page 61 for some ideas). Wet foods are better because they increase water intake. You can also add water to its food to increase water intake. Adding a sprinkle of salt to its water may encourage some cats to drink; however, you should not do this if your cat has been diagnosed with heart or kidney problems. Adding a few drops of brine from a drop of a tin of tuna to its water bowl may help encourage water intake.

If your cat is not at all interested in food and water, you can try to carefully syringe either some pureed food, water or a balanced electrolyte solution into its mouth. Most cats require 200–250 mL water per day from their food and drinking water combined. If your cat continues to be anorexic, depressed or has any vomiting or diarrhoea you should take it to see your veterinarian.

Constipation

Constipation is the inability to pass stools normally, causing a build-up. This can occur secondary to dehydration, especially if the cat has kidney problems (kidney or renal insufficiency or failure) and becomes dehydrated because the faeces become too dry (see Dehydration page 64). Constipation is more common in overweight and inactive cats or cats with reduced mobility. Excessive hair in the faeces can also cause constipation. This is more likely to occur in long-haired cats. Grooming and possibly clipping your cat regularly can be beneficial. Constipation can also occur in cats with itchy skin conditions who over groom. Working with your veterinarian to manage any skin conditions can help prevent over grooming and constipation.

Constipation can also be due to an underlying problem such as motility problems of the colon (large bowel), for example megacolon, or blockages due to tumours or a narrowed pelvis due to previous injuries. Signs of constipation include passing reduced amounts of faeces and straining to defecate, often with yowling. Any stools that are passed are usually very hard and dry and are often large. Occasionally constipated cats will pass diarrhoea around impacted faeces, which can be confusing. Constipated cats will also sometimes vomit and this usually happens when they are straining to pass faeces.

If you suspect that your cat is constipated you can give one teaspoon of psyllium husk every 12 hours. This can be added to your cat's food if it will eat it. Alternatively you can suspend this in several millilitres of water and administer it via a syringe. Psyllium capsules are now available from pharmacists and supermarkets. You can also purchase large gelatin capsules that you can fill with psyllium yourself and then administer orally to the cat. Gelatin capsules are available from your veterinarian or a pharmacist. Instead of or in addition to psyllium, you can administer a laxative designed for cats. Do not administer laxatives designed for people. Increasing your cat's water intake may also be beneficial (see Dehydration on page 65). If there is no improvement in 48 hours, or if your cat has any other sign of illness including a poor appetite, lethargy, depression or vomiting, you should take it to your veterinarian.

If you suspect that your cat is constipated, you should NOT give it plain liquid paraffin or mineral oil. Cats' throats do not handle these substances well and they can aspirate it, which can cause a severe pneumonia.

Note that straining to urinate can sometimes look like straining to defecate and can be confused with constipation. Constipation is rarely an emergency unless it is severe and prolonged. A urinary obstruction will initially cause straining to urinate unproductively and is a medical emergency so if you suspect this you should take your cat to your veterinarian (see Lower Urinary Problems on page 69).

Straining to defecate can sometimes indicate inflammation in the large bowel or colon (colitis). If this is the case, the cat usually passes small amounts of soft faeces regularly. There may be fresh blood or mucus (which looks like jelly) in the stools. If this is severe, persistent or recurrent you should take your cat to see your veterinarian.

Hypothermia

Due to their desert origins, cats are relatively resistant to heat stroke or hyperthermia. Although heat stroke can occur, it is rare and elevations in body temperature (greater than $39.5°C$) are usually due to fevers. If you suspect that your cat has a fever or hyperthermia you should take it to your veterinarian to have this investigated and treated. On the other hand, cats are prone to a reduced body temperature (less than $37.5°C$), or hypothermia, due to many different conditions and disease processes. You should measure your cat's body temperature rectally to help detect hypothermia.

Hypothermia can occur in cats that have been exposed to cold or wet weather. It is especially likely to occur when it is also windy. Hypothermia can also occur when cats fall into cold water. Sometimes cats inadvertently allow themselves to become exposed to the elements because something else serious has happened to them such as tick paralysis or a snakebite. Many other diseases such as heart disease or very advanced infections can cause the body temperature to drop. Small kittens, older or very thin cats are more susceptible to hypothermia.

Regardless of the cause for the reduced body temperature, hypothermia is relatively easy to detect rectally. Your cat is cold if its rectal temperature is below 37.5°C. The condition of your cat will vary with how cold it is, how long it has been cold and any disease processes that are causing it to become cold. If it is weak, depressed, collapsed or having difficulty breathing you should take it to see your veterinarian immediately.

Hypothermia starts to become a more serious concern below 36°C and if your cat's temperature is below this for any reason you should take it to see your veterinarian. You can start re-warming your cat on the way to the veterinary hospital.

If your cat's temperature is between 37 and 37.5°C you probably do not need to do anything to actively warm it, at least initially. You should take it to a warm place and perhaps cover it with a blanket. If its temperature is below 37°C you should check them for signs of shock as described in Assessing the Feline Emergency Patient on page 41.

You should be more aggressive with your warming efforts the colder your cat is. If your cat is wet you should dry its coat with a warm hair drier held at least 30 centimetres away from it. You can also wrap your cat in a blanket or towel or use a 'space' blanket if you have one. Bubble wrap packing material is a good insulator that you can wrap a cold cat in, especially around its paws. You can also warm your cat with radiant or blow heaters.

You can also use surface heating devices such as hot water bottles, electric blankets or electric heat pads. These should not be too hot and you should be able to hold them against your skin without any discomfort. This will be a maximum of 41°C for any of these heating devices. Any heating device should not come into direct contact with your cat's skin as they can cause significant burns. Instead, you should have several layers of blankets or towels between the heat source and your cat's skin. Such surface heating devices may work better if they are placed against areas such as the groin region and possibly the armpits. These areas have good blood supply and this helps raise the core body temperature. Warming other more peripheral areas can actually be detrimental, at least initially. You should change hot water bottles once they are not warm to touch because at this point they will not be effective. If your cat is not tolerating being warmed up and keeps moving away from any heat source you should take it to your veterinarian to have its condition investigated and treated.

You should check your cat's body temperature every 30 minutes to an hour to see if your warming efforts are effective. If not you should consider taking it to your veterinarian. If you are transporting your cat you should have the car's heater on high.

Re-warming a cold cat too quickly can sometimes be harmful; your aim should be to raise its temperature by around 1°C per hour. You can stop warming your cat once its temperature has reached 38.0°C. Once you have increased its temperature you should continue to monitor it to check if it drops again. Because hypothermia may be due to an underlying illness, you should take your cat to your veterinarian to have this investigated.

Lower Urinary Tract Problems

Lower urinary tract problems are relatively common in cats. These are diseases of the bladder and urethra. These problems are caused by a variety of diseases, some of which are more common than others. Regardless of the cause, the signs of these problems are very similar and you cannot differentiate these problems based on what your cat is doing. The most important thing to try to determine is whether or not there is a urinary tract obstruction because this is a medical emergency.

Although any cause of lower urinary tract signs can occur in any cat, the most common cause for lower urinary tract disease in cats is a condition called sterile interstitial cystitis or idiopathic (of unknown cause) cystitis. The cause of this is unknown but may be due to a viral infection. This condition can be triggered by stress such as major changes like moving, changes in the weather, new animals or people in the household, people leaving the household or new cats in the neigbourhood. It is more common in overweight indoor cats that have sedentary lifestyles. Long-haired cats are also more commonly affected as well as highly strung or anxious cats. Cats are most likely to have their first episode when they are less than eight years old. It is rare for cats to have their first episode when they are older than eight years old unless they have another disease such as hyperthyroidism. Lower urinary disease can be a recurrent problem in some cats. It is NOT usually due to a bacterial infection and in fact bacterial infections are very rare in otherwise healthy cats less than eight years old. They are more common in female cats, cats with diabetes (see Diabetes on page 96), or cats with kidney problems (see Kidney Problems on page 100).

Crystals in the urine or stones in the bladder can also cause lower urinary tract signs. These can be often dietary related but are now far less common because large efforts are made to ensure commercial cat diets have balanced levels of minerals. Bladder tumours can also cause lower urinary tract signs and are more common in older cats.

Signs of lower urinary tract disease include urinating small amounts frequently. The cat may strain to urinate and spend a large time while only passing a small amount of urine. It may cry or yowl while urinating due to pain and frustration. Cats with lower urinary tract problems will often urinate in unusual places such as sinks, baths, showers and pot plants. There may be evidence of blood in the urine. The urine may be either reddened or there may be drops of fresh blood. Male cats may lick their penis a lot, making it irritated. If your cat has lower urinary tract problems it may be generally depressed, in pain and may have a reduced appetite. Cats with urinary tract infections may have very smelly urine in addition to the other signs of cystitis.

You need to determine if your cat has a urinary tract obstruction or simply irritation causing the signs. A urinary obstruction will cause the waste products normally excreted in the urine to build up in the blood. This can cause severe electrolyte abnormalities that can affect the heart's rhythm and function and the blood to become too acidic. These changes can be life threatening.

Urinary tract obstructions are much more common in male cats than female cats. It can be quite difficult to determine whether your cat has a urinary tract obstruction because some of the signs are very similar to non-obstructive lower urinary tract disease. These signs including straining to urinate unproductively and painfully and licking their penis excessively causing it to become swollen and irritated. After several hours of unproductive straining cats with a urinary tract obstruction will often give up trying to urinate and will become progressively more lethargic and depressed. Eventually they will collapse.

The bladder of a cat with a urinary tract obstruction will be very large and firm. I do not recommend that you try to feel your cat's bladder because there is a chance that you will rupture it due to the pressure. Leave this examination to your veterinarian. If you have to pick your cat up, pick it up from behind its hind limbs to prevent putting excessive pressure on its bladder.

If there is any doubt about whether your cat has a urinary tract obstruction, you should take it to your veterinarian to be investigated and treated. In the interim, if your cat has signs of lower urinary tract disease but is passing urine, the most beneficial things that you can do for it are to increase its water intake and to encourage it to urinate more often. You can increase your cat's water intake by feeding a wet or canned diet rather than dry food. If your cat tolerates it you can add some water to its food. It should have multiple water bowls around the house in quiet areas. You can add a sprinkle of salt or a few drops of brine from a tin of tuna to some of its water bowls as this will encourage some cats to drink. Note that you should not add additional salt to your cat's food or water if it has been diagnosed with heart or kidney problems.

Your cat should have multiple litter trays available in various quiet, stress-free locations around the house. It can also be helpful to use different types of litter but you should leave its normal litter as a choice because taking this away can be stressful.

Your cat's condition should be investigated by your veterinarian so more specific treatments can be prescribed.

Convulsions, Fits and Seizures

Convulsions or fits are usually called seizures by veterinarians. Unlike the situation in dogs and people, these are relatively uncommon in cats. They can have many causes but because epilepsy is very rare in cats, most other causes of seizures are due to serious underlying disease. These causes can be due to problems outside the brain such as poisons, low blood glucose or liver problems. They can also be due to a problem within the brain itself such as infections with protozoa, fungus or rarely bacteria or tumours. Seizures can be generalised and cause unconsciousness, rigid limbs, continuous violent limb movements or 'paddling', salivation, or frothing at the mouth and possibly urination or defecation. Partial seizures vary greatly in their presentation, but usually involve involuntary movements such as facial twitching or changes in behaviour while the cat remains conscious.

Sometimes a seizure may just be an episode of staring into space. Prior to a seizure, a period called the aura, the cat may be anxious and behave abnormally. Similarly once a cat has recovered from a seizure, it may be disoriented and is often very hungry or thirsty. It may even appear blind, behave very strangely and sometimes seem demented. This is called the post-ictal period and can last for hours to days, even after only a short seizure.

Seizures can be very upsetting for onlookers especially if it is the first time that you have seen your cat have one. If your cat has a seizure for the first time, the cause for this may or may not be obvious. Conversely, there may be evidence that your cat has ingested a toxin, in which case you should take it to your veterinarian immediately. Seizures may occur due to low blood sugar or hypoglycaemia in diabetic cats that have had an insulin overdose (see Diabetes on page 97). It can also occur in young kittens which have not eaten regularly enough or have been vomiting. If you suspect that the seizure has been caused by low blood sugar, you should rub some honey or another sweet substance on the cat's gums, being very careful avoid being bitten, and take it to your veterinarian immediately. If your cat recovers from the seizure, offer it a high protein meal such as cat food or meat and then take it to your veterinarian. When the cause for the seizure is not obvious you should take your cat to your veterinarian as soon as possible.

Regardless of the cause of the seizure you should move any objects such as furniture away from the cat so that it does not hurt itself. You should not try to comfort or hold the cat as seizuring cats are usually unconscious and the movements are involuntary. Similarly do not try to rouse the cat. A seizure will last as long as it is going to last and talking to, yelling at or shaking the cat will not stop it. You should also not put your hand in a seizuring cat's mouth as the cat may bite you involuntarily. Cats rarely swallow their tongue or even bite it. You can start to comfort the cat once it starts to recover.

If your cat has been diagnosed with a seizure disorder such as epilepsy and perhaps is on anticonvulsant medication, a seizure may not be as surprising or upsetting and the cause is usually more obvious. There may be less urgency to see your veterinarian. However, you should take your cat to a veterinarian if a seizure lasts more than 90 seconds. Seizures typically feel much longer than they actually are so you should time them. Sometimes seizures will be continuous without the cat recovering and this can be very dangerous as it can cause the body to overheat and damage the brain. You should take your cat to a veterinarian if it has more than two seizures in one day, especially if they are in quick succession. If your cat is having a continuous seizure or is having seizures one after another, you should try to keep it cool while you transport it to your veterinarian. To do this, spray its coat with cool water or cover it with a wet towel and turn your car's air-conditioning onto maximum or at least open the windows. Closely monitor your cat's temperature as it may then become hypothermic and require warming (see Hypothermia on page 67).

It is also very important to make the environment as safe as possible for a cat with a seizure disorder so that it does not injure itself during a seizure or during the post-ictal period when it is very disoriented. Swimming pools and other bodies of water are especially dangerous as a cat can drown during a seizure. Cliffs and balconies and other heights where a cat may fall are also dangerous. These areas should be secured so that a cat with a seizure disorder cannot access them. You should not try to give any oral medication to your cat while it is having a seizure.

Poisoning

Cats are fastidious creatures which, unlike dogs or children, rarely eat poisonous substances. There are several toxic substances that are attractive to cats for some reason and they may eat them. These include ethylene glycol or antifreeze, plants of the lily (*Liliaceae*) family and benzalkalonium chloride, a disinfectant in common cleaning products. Despite their normally selective nature, cats occasionally ingest other poisons: not all of these can be listed here. If you are concerned that your cat has or MAY have ingested a poison you should call or take it to your veterinarian and you should call a poisons information service. You should try to estimate how much of the toxin your cat has ingested. Estimating how much is left in the packet may help with this. You should also take the packet to your veterinarian so they can identify the toxin and its concentration in the product.

It is not uncommon for cats to become poisoned by well-meaning owners or carers who administer human medication to cats. Cats are around one fifteenth the weight of the average human so they require much smaller doses of medication. In addition, cats are especially sensitive to several medications: including paracetamol, aspirin and medication of the non-steroidal anti-inflammatory drug family (NSAID) such as ibuprofen and naproxen. These drugs can be very harmful and potentially fatal to cats so you should not administer these to your cat. If you realise that you have inadvertently administered a potentially toxic substance to your cat it may be appropriate to induce vomiting if there is going to be a delay in taking your cat to a veterinarian. Similarly, some anti-flea or tick products specifically designed for dogs that contain synthetic pyrethroids can be harmful to cats. These products are typically labelled for use in dogs only and should never be used for cats.

Cats are secretive animals so they have usually ingested a poison long before you realise. The first thing you notice is the effect of the poison. This often means that any first aid efforts should be directed towards supportive care and taking the cat to a veterinarian rather than decontamination efforts such as inducing vomiting, because this is unlikely to be beneficial so long after the ingestion. However, if the ingestion was known to have occurred within the last 2–4 hours, decontamination by inducing vomiting and administering activated charcoal may be appropriate.

Decontamination

Inducing vomiting may be appropriate in the first instance in certain not-caustic or non-corrosive toxicities. Vomiting can help expel toxins from the stomach and reduce their absorption. A veterinarian may perform a gastric lavage (stomach 'pump') and an enema if more advanced measures are required. As stated above, poisonings are often identified too long after ingestion for vomiting to be of significant benefit. It is also important to consider that some veterinarians believe that vomiting is not of significant benefit in treating feline intoxications. Administering activated charcoal can be beneficial as this binds some toxins in the stomach and intestines. Examples of when these decontamination measures may be beneficial include poisoning by lily, ethylene glycol or antifreeze, non-steroidal anti-inflammatory drugs, aspirin, paracetamol and rat and mice bait. Decontamination is ideally instituted as soon as possible. Vomiting may be beneficial for up to 2–4 hours after ingestion. For some poisons, activated charcoal administration may be beneficial for up to 24 hours after ingestion.

If there is going to be a significant delay in seeing a veterinarian, a safe way to induce vomiting is to administer 1 teaspoon (or 2–4 mIL) of 3 per cent hydrogen peroxide by mouth. Once measured, you can draw the hydrogen peroxide into a syringe or a turkey blaster and administer into the mouth. If your cat does not vomit after 10–15 minutes you can repeat this dose once. If it is still not effective you should take your cat to a veterinarian. Stronger solutions can be diluted to 3 per cent. For example, you have to dilute a 10 per cent solution by adding one part of a 10 per cent solution to two parts water. Solutions of hydrogen peroxide at a concentration greater than 3 per cent should not be used as they can cause irritation to the food pipe and stomach. Please note that occasionally hydrogen peroxide of any concentration can be irritating to the lining of the food pipe (oesophagus) and stomach and very occasionally this is severe. You should use this technique with caution. Once you have induced vomiting it will generally continue for several minutes at most and then will stop on its own accord. Occasionally vomiting will be prolonged and you will need to take your cat to a veterinarian for this. Regardless of whether or not the toxin is recovered you should take your cat to your veterinarian as dangerous amounts may still be in the stomach or already absorbed.

There are certain circumstances where it is definitely NOT appropriate to induce vomiting as this can be detrimental. You should not induce vomiting if your cat:

- is already vomiting
- is overly weak or collapsed
- is hyperexciteable
- is seizuring
- has ingested a caustic or corrosive substance such as benzalkalonium chloride or bleach.

Vomiting also has the potential to worsen heart conditions so if your cat has a heart condition you should not induce vomiting. In addition if you are ever unsure if inducing vomiting at home is appropriate you should discuss this with your veterinarian or a poisons information centre (see page 111 for Emergency Contacts).

Some people recommend using ipecac syrup in cats; however, this is not particularly effective and the ipecac itself can be toxic to cats. I do not recommend using ipecac to induce vomiting in cats. Similarly some people recommend administering large amounts of table salt. If the cat does not vomit this then it has the potential to cause salt toxicity and so I do not recommend using salt to induce vomiting.

Activated charcoal can be beneficial in binding poisons within the bowel to help prevent them being absorbed. This is available as tablets and liquid suspensions and should be given at a dose of 4–12 g per cat. This works out to be 12–40 300mg tablets, which is a little impractical. It is probably best for your veterinarian to administer this if it is necessary as they can also use more effective forms and methods. However, if there is going to be a significant delay in seeing a veterinarian you should administer this. Activated charcoal should be given after you have induced vomiting and the vomiting has stopped. If vomiting has not been induced because the toxin was ingested too long ago, activated charcoal can be given as soon as possible after ingestion. Activated charcoal should not be given to animals which are vomiting. It should also not be given to animals that are convulsing, hyperexciteable, overly weak or collapsed. Activated charcoal should not be given with food as this will bind to it and reduce its effectiveness. Activated charcoal will also bind to other medications and prevent them from being absorbed so it should not be given within one hour before or two hours after other important medications. Burnt toast is not a substitute for activated charcoal as it is ineffective.

Lilies

The leaves and flowers from plants of the lily (*Liliaceae*) family including Asian, Day, Easter, Glory, Japanese Show, Peace, Red, Rubrum, Stargazer, Tiger and Wood lilies are highly poisonous to cats. For some reason cats, especially young cats, are prone to ingesting them and becoming intoxicated. All parts of the plant are considered poisonous including flowers, leaves, pollen and the stems. Only small amounts of the plant are required to cause poisoning. Even a kitten mouthing a plant should be considered a serious and potentially fatal ingestion.

Signs of lily toxicity usually start within several hours of exposure and include depression, anorexia and vomiting. Within 24–72 hours acute kidney or renal failure can develop, which causes abdominal (kidney) pain and a marked reduction in urine production or complete cessation of production. With time affected cats will become increasingly depressed. This is a life threatening condition and even with the most aggressive treatment many cats die from this. If you suspect that your cat has, or even MAY have ingested any lilies or is suffering from lily toxicity, you should take it to your veterinarian immediately as early detection and treatment is vital. If there is going to be a delay you should start decontamination procedures unless there is a reason not to (see Poisoning page 75). If your cat has recently ingested Peace Lilies (also known as White Lilies) you should not induce vomiting, instead administer a small amount of milk or yoghurt and take your cat to your veterinarian immediately.

Automotive radiator antifreeze/coolant —ethylene glycol

Just like lilies, ethylene glycol or antifreeze ingestion can cause acute kidney or renal failure in cats. Cats may find antifreeze or coolant that has leaked from a car radiator. Ideally cats should not have access to areas where such spills could occur. Any puddles should be regularly cleaned up. For some reason cats like to ingest this substance. This is interesting because it is considered a sweet substance and cats have a reduced ability to taste sweet substances. Ingestion of even only a few millilitres can be a fatal dose. If you suspect that your cat has or even MAY have ingested ethylene glycol, you should take it to your veterinarian immediately.

Signs of intoxication initially include incoordination (a drunken appearance) and depression. These signs can occur within 30 minutes of ingestion and can last up to 12 hours. Signs can even progress to a coma and death within this time. From 12–24 hours after ingestion there can be rapid breathing and depression. Usually within 24–72 hours of ingestion there can be signs of kidney or renal failure including anorexia, vomiting, abdominal (kidney) pain and a marked reduction in or complete cessation of urine production. With time the cat will become increasingly depressed. This is a life threatening condition even with the most aggressive treatment. If you suspect that your cat has or even MAY have ingested ethylene glycol or is suffering from ethylene glycol toxicity you should take it to your veterinarian immediately. If there is going to be a delay you should start decontamination procedures unless there is a reason not to, as explained under Poisoning on page 75.

Paracetamol

Paracetamol is a common over-the-counter painkiller for people. Cats are very sensitive to paracetamol and even tiny doses can be poisonous. Also, cats break paracetamol down into toxic compounds. These compounds can change the oxygen carrying compound in red blood cells, haemoglobin, so that it cannot carry oxygen. It changes the haemoglobin to a brown compound called methaemoglobin, which can make the cat's lips and gums turn brown. These changes can cause serious reductions in blood oxygen levels resulting in rapid and laboured breathing. These signs can occur within 2–6 hours of ingestion. Cats with paracetamol toxicity will often develop a swollen face and may repeatedly paw at their face. They may also develop swollen paws. Other signs of paracetamol toxicity include lethargy, depression and hypothermia (see Hypothermia on page 67). Paracetamol toxicity can also cause significant liver damage.

Unfortunately people often give paracetamol to cats when they are unwell and it can be even more harmful in these circumstances.

Paracetamol toxicity is a very serious condition. If you have inadvertently given any amount of paracetamol to your cat, you should take it to your veterinarian. If there is going to be a delay and your cat is not yet showing any signs of toxicity, you should start decontamination procedures unless there is a reason not to, as outlined in Poisoning on page 75. You should not start decontamination if your cat is already showing signs of toxicity.

Non-steroidal anti-inflammatory drugs and aspirin

Non-steroidal anti-inflammatory drugs (NSAIDs) are another common class of readily available over-the-counter pain relief medications for people.

These include ibuprofen, naproxen, indomethacin and diclofenac. There are also products designed for use in dogs such as meloxicam, carprofen and tolfenamic acid. These are sometimes cautiously used in cats. Some veterinary NSAID preparations are flavoured and as a result cats may find them attractive. Be careful to store these drugs out of your cat's reach. Aspirin is another drug similar to NSAIDs that can also be toxic. Cats are particularly sensitive to NSAIDs and aspirin and can easily become intoxicated. There are some veterinary formulations of NSAIDs that are safer for use in cats and you should discuss this with your veterinarian. Even these drugs can still cause problems, especially if they are used inappropriately or if overdoses are given. Unfortunately people often give NSAIDs or aspirin to cats when they are unwell and it can be even more harmful in these circumstances.

NSAIDs can cause gastric ulcers, which can lead to severe bleeding. They can also cause kidney damage and even kidney or renal failure. Signs of toxicity include lethargy or depression, anorexia, vomiting (possibly with fresh blood or evidence of digested blood which looks like coffee grounds), black faeces, pale gums, increased water intake and urination or reduced or ceased urine output.

If you have inadvertently given a NSAID, aspirin or an overdose of one of these drugs you should take your cat to your veterinarian. If there is going to be a delay you should start decontamination procedures unless there is a reason not to as outlined in Poisoning on page 75.

Rat and mice bait

Rat and mice baits or rodenticides are very dangerous for cats. They have been designed so that they are attractive to rats so invariably they are also attractive to cats. By far the most common type of bait is one which blocks vitamin K recycling. Vitamin K is vital for the body to make the factors needed for the blood to clot. As a result this type of bait stops the blood clotting and causes excessive bleeding. These products are extremely potent and even eating a rat killed by the toxin can be enough to cause poisoning. Your cat is therefore potentially at risk if you see it eating a rat or find the remains of a half-eaten rat. Bleeding is not immediate and instead it usually occurs from 36–48 hours after ingestion. In some cases signs may not be present until up to one week after exposure. Bleeding may be internal so it may not be obvious, so if you suspect that your cat has ingested rodenticide but appears normal, it is still at grave risk and you need to take it to see your veterinarian.

You should take your cat to your veterinarian so that it can receive the antidote which is a special form of vitamin K and any other supportive treatments considered necessary. As your cat is at risk of bleeding easily you should handle it very gently and keep it calm. You should also feed it only soft food. Because new forms of rodenticides are very long acting, a long-treatment course is likely to be necessary. If the baits were laid by professionals, you should contact them to find out the exact substance that they used.

Another type of rodenticide is based on a massive overdose of vitamin D, which then causes blood calcium to rise to toxic levels. Signs are seen 12–36 hours after ingestion and include progressive depression, increased thirst and urination, and ultimately death. This second type of rodenticide is now quite rare and your cat is most likely to get exposure from access to old packets that have been stored.

If your cat has eaten a poisoned dead rat or mouse, the poison may have been laid by one of your neighbours. It is important to find out if it is likely that your cat has been poisoned. Be as diplomatic as possible when asking your neighbours about this. If you are aggressive and accusatory they are much more likely to deny everything and not having this information may put your cat's life at risk.

If you suspect that your cat has ingested a rodenticide you should take it to your veterinarian immediately. If there is going to be a delay you should start decontamination procedures unless there is a reason not to as outlined in Poisoning on page 75.

Synthetic pyrethroids—permethrin

Some flea or tick products such as washes, rinses, collars, sprays and top spot preparations contain synthetic pyrethroids. The most common active ingredient is permethrin. These products are usually labelled as for use in dogs only and cats are especially sensitive to them. They are readily absorbed though the skin. Signs usually occur within a few hours of exposure, but occasionally the signs will be delayed by up to 24 hours.

Permethrin poisoning causes severe muscle tremors especially of the facial muscles and ear. These can be very distressing for the cat and for onlookers. Muscle tremors can lead to an elevated body temperature, which can be very dangerous. The muscles can start to break down releasing a redish brown pigment that discolours the urine and can then damage the kidneys. In extreme cases permethrin poisoning can lead to continuous seizuring (see Convulsions, Fits and Seizures on page 72). Other signs include increased salivation, drooling and occasionally vomiting.

Permethrin poisoning is very serious and if you suspect that your cat has become intoxicated with a synthetic pyrethroid such as permethrin, you should take it to your veterinarian immediately. If there is going to be a significant delay in this, you should carefully try to wash the product off its skin. You should do this in a sink of tepid water or under warm running water. You should be careful to keep the cat's head above water at all times. Using a gentle shampoo can be very helpful. Sometimes a cat is too agitated by their condition and cannot be washed without sedation or even anaesthesia. You should take it to your veterinarian immediately. Do NOT bath your cat if it has severe muscle tremors, is hyperexciteable or is seizuring, has difficulty breathing or is overly dull and depressed; instead take it to your veterinarian immediately.

Do NOT use any products on your cat that are not labelled for use in cats. Always read product labels carefully and use them on your cat only as directed.

Washing your cat should help reduce its body temperature significantly. If its body temperature is still above 39.5°C you can continue to cool it using fans and damp towels. When you transport your cat to your veterinarian you should have the air-conditioning on. Once a cat has been cooled and starts to recover from the signs of poisoning, it can become cold and require warming as hypothermia can increase the degree of the toxicity and prolong your cat's recovery (see Hypothermia on page 67). Cats with permethrin toxicity often require extensive supportive care and you should take it to your veterinarian as soon as possible. Do NOT induce vomiting or administer activated charcoal.

Flea and tick products that have organophosphates as their active ingredient which are labelled for use in dogs only can also be very poisonous to cats. Examples of the active ingredients in these products include fenthion, diazinon, chlorpyrifos and temephos. These compounds can also be found in products designed for cats and these products rarely cause a problem when used as directed by the label.

Benzalkalonium chloride and bleach

Benzalkalonium chloride is a quaternary ammonium chloride compound that is commonly found in disinfectant detergents. When it pools and then dries on a surface such as a floor or the inside of a cat carry cage it forms crystals. Cats find this substance appealing and will lick and ingest the crystals. This substance is very corrosive and causes severe damage to the mouth, tongue and throat. Signs include difficulty or pain when eating or anorexia, profuse salivation, excessive swallowing and depression.

Bleach is another corrosive substance that cats sometimes lick, causing similar signs. The damage to the lining on the mouth can be severe and usually requires aggressive treatment by your veterinarian. If you discover your cat ingesting these substances or suspect that it has, you can use a syringe filled with water to carefully flush its mouth out several times. Offering or syringing milk or egg whites into your cat's mouth can be soothing and provide some relief. However, if the problem is serious enough, your veterinarian may need to anaesthetise your cat to examine it, flush its mouth and possibly place a feeding tube for longer term management. So unless there will be a significant delay (greater than two hours) before you see your veterinarian, you should not give your cat anything but water. Do NOT induce vomiting or administer activated charcoal.

Ticks, Bites and Insect Stings

Tick paralysis

Tick paralysis is caused by the paralysis tick, which only occurs in bushy coastal areas along the eastern seaboard of Australia. Ticks are most prevalent from spring to autumn; however, paralysis can occur at any time of year. Other types of ticks can cause skin irritation and itchiness. Some ticks will transmit serious infectious diseases.

Paralysis ticks will jump onto cats then attach themselves by burrowing their mouth parts into the skin. They can attach anywhere, even in the ears, on the lips or around the anus. However, they most commonly attach on the front half of the cat. Fortunately most cats are good at removing ticks themselves when they groom before the tick can cause a problem. In my experience, the most common place for ticks to attach is around the shoulder region because cats have difficulty reaching this area. Cats can have multiple ticks attached at once. Occasionally numerous tiny juvenile ticks can attach and cause a problem.

Once the tick is attached it stays there feeding on the host's blood. During this time the tick also secretes a toxin from its saliva into the cat. This toxin causes the connection between the nerves and the muscles throughout the body to become disrupted, resulting in weakness and ultimately paralysis. This is not just limited to the muscles on the outside of the body but also those inside such as those involved in swallowing in the mouth and the food pipe.

As a very general rule, for a tick to cause a cat a problem, it either has to be quite large (greater than four millimetres long) or be attached for at least four days. However, there can be marked variation in the potency of the tick and also the individual cat's susceptibility to tick paralysis, which may vary from season to season. Cats that are affected by tick paralysis will start to show signs of weakness and become uncoordinated. This usually starts in the hind limbs and gradually progresses forward until the cat collapses. The toxin will also affect the voice box so the cat may have a different meow or may not be able to meow at all. This may also cause affected cats to grunt when they breathe out or are picked up.

If ticks are attached near the eyes they can make the eyelids paralysed and stop the cat from blinking which can cause the eyes to dry out and become damaged. You can test your cat's ability to blink by touching each of its eyelids just next to the nose. Your cat should be able to close its eye completely. If it is not able to do this, applying artificial or synthetic tears regularly can help keep the eyes lubricated.

Because the tick's poison also causes weakness and dilation of the food pipe, affected cats may retch and regurgitate their food, water or just frothy fluid. One serious complication of this is aspiration of fluid or food into the lungs, which causes pneumonia. Affected cats may also have difficulty swallowing, which can cause fluid to build up in the mouth and throat which can make them choke.

Tick paralysis often causes breathing difficulty. If the paralysis becomes too advanced and the muscles involved with breathing become too weak, the cat may not be able to breathe sufficiently or at all. Cats become very distressed by not being able to move and this agitation will increase their oxygen requirements and further contribute to their difficulty breathing. Tick paralysis is progressive and potentially fatal.

Paralysis ticks can be identified by their grey body and their legs close to their head. The position of the legs is the paralysis tick's most distinguishing feature. Unlike other adult ticks, paralysis ticks have one pair of brown legs closest to their head, then two pairs of white legs and then

Paralysis tick

one pair of brown legs closest to their body. Very small ticks or nymph or larval forms can be very difficult to identify. Other types of ticks, such as the bush tick, do not cause paralysis but can cause itchiness and irritation and may transmit diseases.

If your cat lives in or visits an area where paralysis ticks are present, you should regularly search it thoroughly. Clipping a long-haired cat's coat short, especially during the tick season, makes performing tick searches much easier. To perform a tick search, work your fingers through its coat and down to the skin and then systematically massage your fingers over the entire body. You should concentrate on the cat's front half as this is where they are more likely to occur. Attached ticks are firmly attached and feel like a hard, smooth, round irregularity on the surface of the skin. Make sure you check the edge of the lips, in skin folds and in the ears. If you think that you have found one, part the fur to have a look at it. Nipples, warts and other bumps on the skin are often mistaken for ticks and you should not attempt to remove them. Sometimes the tick has already become detached by the time that you are performing a search in which case you may only find a crater where a tick has been attached.

No product absolutely prevents ticks from attaching and causing paralysis so regular searches are vital to avoid tick paralysis. However, it can be useful to use a safe product to help prevent tick attachment. Spot-on or tablet form products are probably the most convenient in cats and you

Always ensure that any tick repelling product you use is safe for use on cats.

should discuss this with your veterinarian. If you find a tick, you should use a tick remover to detach it from the skin if you feel comfortable doing so. There are several types of tick removers.

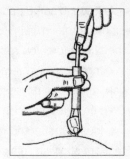

One type of remover resembles a pair of spring-loaded tweezers that are opened and then closed onto the tick where it attaches to the skin. Be careful not to grasp the body of the tick as this risks squeezing more of the toxin into the skin. The device is then twisted on its axis until the tick detaches.

Removing a tick with a tweezer-type remover.

The sickle-shaped or hook-type tick remover has a fork at one end. The fork is placed around where the tick is attached. You then twist the device until the tick breaks free from the skin.

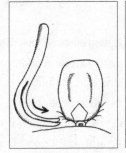

Removing a tick with a hook-type remover.

Another type of remover is a shaft with a small lasso on one end that wraps around the tick's head. You align the shaft perpendicular to the skin and start twisting it on its axis until the tick is removed.

If you do not have a proper tick remover, you can use a pair of tweezers to grasp it at the skin level, being careful not to squeeze on the tick's body. Then gently lever it off, rocking back and forth.

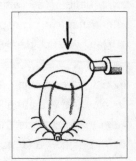

Removing a tick with a lasso-type remover.

If you leave the tick's head embedded in the skin, a reaction may develop at the site and cause itchiness. The remainder of the tick should fall out of its own accord in 2–3 days. If your cat is overly itchy or there is a very red, swollen reaction, you should take your cat to a veterinarian so that it can be removed.

Although some people suggest applying tick treatments, alcohol, mineral oil or petroleum jelly to the tick, I do not recommend applying anything to the tick before you remove it. You should also not try to burn the tick.

Once you have removed the tick, see if you can identify it as a paralysis tick. If it is a paralysis tick you should seek veterinary attention for your cat. Even once a paralysis tick has been removed it is possible for a cat that was previously unaffected to later start to show signs of tick paralysis. Also, cats that are showing signs of paralysis can deteriorate further even after the tick has been removed. Many people do not seek veterinary attention after removing a tick from their cat. If you choose not to, put the tick in a well-sealed container so that if your cat develops a problem your veterinarian can later identify the tick.

Many people who have removed ticks from their cat choose not to see a veterinarian when their cat is only mildly affected by the poison, say just a little bit wobbly in the hindquarters. In my opinion this is dangerous because of the risk of deterioration and all cats showing signs of tick paralysis should be seen by a veterinarian. Many of these cats would go on to recover without treatment, but I don't think that it is worth the risk.

If you suspect that your cat has tick paralysis you can reduce the risk of complications by withholding food and water until you can see a veterinarian. This is especially important if the cat is regurgitating.

Cats with tick paralysis often suffer hypothermia. If you suspect your cat has tick paralysis you should take its temperature. If it is below 37.5°C you should start warming it as described in Hypothermia on page 68. Some people believe that cats with tick paralysis should be kept cold as warming them may stimulate the poison. This is false and can actually exacerbate their condition and slow their recovery. However, cats with tick paralysis should not be overheated as this will stress them and cause further difficulty breathing. If your cat's temperature is greater than 39.5°C you can use a fan or air-conditioner to try to cool it down gently.

On the way to the veterinary hospital you should make sure that your cat is breathing well. If your cat is breathing noisily or is gagging and retching it may have excessive secretions in its mouth. You can try to remove these with a cloth but be careful not to get bitten. You can also elevate its hindquarters slightly so that these secretions drain out of the mouth. If your cat is very badly paralysed and on the way to the veterinary clinic its breathing becomes very weak and shallow, its gums develop a blue tinge or it stops breathing, you will have to start mouth-to-nose breathing as described in Assessing the Feline Emergency Patient on page 40. If your cat's heart stops then you may also have to perform CPR as described on page 42.

Insect sting and bite allergies

Sometimes when cats are bitten by insects, most notably bees, they have an allergic or hypersensitivity reaction. Sometimes the cat becomes intensely itchy and may become agitated. It may also develop hive type lesions on the skin. Other cats develop hard swelling of the face, especially the lips, and sometimes puffy swollen eyelids. The reaction can also make the cat feel generally unwell and it may be quieter than usual. In extreme circumstances the swelling to the tissue in the mouth and throat can become so great that it impairs breathing. These signs can occur immediately after a bite or sting but may take 2–4 hours to develop. Sometimes the delay may be as long as 24–72 hours.

All cats that have suffered such an allergic reaction should be seen by a veterinarian. Treatment may be necessary and the cat may also need to be admitted for observation in case its condition worsens. If there is going to be a delay in getting your cat to a veterinarian or if the cat's swelling is progressing rapidly, it may be appropriate to administer an antihistamine. You should ring your veterinarian to check if this is appropriate and which antihistamine you should use.

You should also search your cat's skin for evidence of an embedded insect sting. You may not be able to find any sting or obvious cause for the reaction but if you do find a sting, you can try to remove it if you feel comfortable doing so. Do not grasp it with your fingers as this risks injecting more of the toxin into the skin. You can use tweezers at the level of the skin

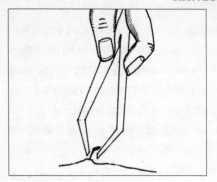

When removing a sting with tweezers avoid squeezing the bulb containing toxins.

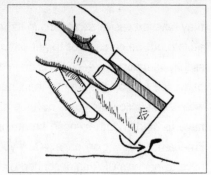

Removing an insect sting using a credit card.

to remove the sting but be careful not to squeeze on the bulb. Instead you could use a stiff piece of cardboard or a credit card by running an edge along the surface of the skin to flick the sting out. You could also use cool compresses on the swollen areas in an attempt to reduce the swelling on your way to your veterinarian.

Similar reactions can also occur after administration of a vaccine or after exposure to certain pollens. Sometimes similar reactions can occur when many tiny juvenile ticks are attached to the skin.

Stink bug (also known as bronze orange, shield, green shield or green vegetable bugs) sprays can cause severe eye pain and damage (see Eye Problems on page 96).

Anaphylaxis

Just as some people are highly allergic to certain insect stings, some cats are extremely sensitive and may suffer anaphylaxis, which is a severe and life threatening allergic reaction. Cats suffering anaphylaxis will become weak, may collapse, and have signs of shock (see Assessing the Feline Emergency Patient on page 41). They may appear nauseous and may vomit. Later they may start straining to defecate or start passing diarrhoea that may be bloody. In extreme circumstances they may have difficulty breathing or stop breathing or their heart may stop. For more information see CPR on page 42 for instructions on resuscitation. If your cat has suffered an episode of anaphylaxis before, you may have been dispensed or prescribed an adrenaline injection pen by your veterinarian. If you feel comfortable administering this, do so according to your veterinarian's instructions. If you suspect that your cat is suffering anaphylaxis, you should take it to your veterinarian immediately.

Snakebites

Snakebites can cause serious illness and even death. Not all snakebites are venomous; however, since some venomous snakebites are potentially fatal, all snakebites should be treated as life threatening. If you see a snake near your cat or your cat playing with or attacking a snake and later find your cat collapsed, vomiting, salivating, trembling, inappropriately urinating or defecating, this is suggestive of a potentially fatal bite. Often cats will seem to recover quickly from this episode but go on to suffer further effects of the envenomation. Different snakes, however, affect cats differently.

After this initial phase major signs of envenomation that may develop are incoordination and progressive weakness, eventually resulting in paralysis. Some snakebites will show a delayed onset of signs, up to several days later. These may include blood in the urine or bleeding due to problems with blood clotting. Sometimes owners will actually see a snake bite their cat. If you are suspicious that your cat has been bitten by a snake you should take your cat to your veterinarian immediately but as quietly as possible. Carry your cat or keep it in a carry cage because exercise will speed up the movement of the venom around the body.

If your cat has collapsed or is starting to become limp and paralysed while you transport it, you should keep your cat sitting up rather than lying on its side. This is because it is easier for it to breathe in this position.

When a cat starts to become paralysed by a snakebite, lots of saliva can build up in the mouth and block its airway so you should elevate its hindquarters so the saliva drains out of the mouth. You can also use a cloth to remove some of it but be careful to avoid being bitten (see Assessing the Feline Emergency Patient on page 39 for more details).

If, during your trip to the veterinary clinic, your cat's breathing becomes very weak and shallow, if its gums develop a blue tinge or it stops breathing, you will have to start mouth-to-nose breathing (see page 40). If its heart stops then you may also have to perform CPR (see page 42). Be gentle when doing this as some snake venoms stop the blood from clotting and chest compressions can cause bleeding.

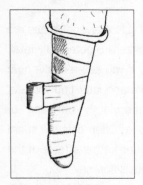

A pressure bandage stops the venom spreading.

If there is going to be a significant delay in getting to a veterinary clinic, and the bite was on a limb, you can apply a pressure bandage to help delay the movement of the toxin from the bite site around the body. This should be applied firmly to help prevent the venom spreading. First apply a layer of cotton-roll dressing. This should start higher on the limb than the bite and continue down to the toes. You should then apply a firm layer of conforming gauze over this. You can either stick the bandage on with adhesive tape or apply a layer of adhesive bandage over this. If you are using adhesive bandage, again start above the bite and continue down towards the toes (see picture). If you do not have any bandaging material you can fashion a pressure bandage out of clothing. Unfortunately snakebites are often impossible to find or are on the cat's face. If this is the case you should just keep your cat as calm and as still as possible while travelling to your veterinarian.

Sneezing, Sniffles and Snuffles

Cats can develop signs of sneezing, sniffling, snuffling, nasal discharge or noisy breathing for many reasons. Possibly the most common cause is the so-called cat flu complex. This can also become complicated by secondary bacterial infections. In a small number of cats chronic infections can result in a condition where sufferers are known as chronic snufflers. Other possible causes of these signs include polyps at the back of the nose, bad dental disease, inhaled foreign bodies such as grass seeds, fungal infections in the nose and nasal cancers.

The cat flu complex is actually caused by a completely different group of viruses than in humans and other animals. The human flu is caused by infection with influenza virus whereas 'cat flu' is caused by infection with either the herpes virus, calicivirus, chlamydia (an unusual bacteria) or a combination of these. To complicate matters cats can become infected with influenza viruses, but this is uncommon. Often cats become infected when they are kittens but they can also be infected later in life. Vaccination can help prevent or reduce the signs of illness. Once a cat is infected it usually carries the disease for life and the signs may reappear during times of stress such as boarding or changes in the household. The most common signs are sneezing, discharge from both nostrils that is usually clear but can become yellow or green if there is a secondary infection. In addition, cats suffering from cat flu may have ulcers in their mouth, which can cause drooling and a reluctance to eat. Cats' appetites are highly dependent on their sense of smell. When their nose is blocked and they cannot smell, many cats stop eating. The cat flu complex can also cause discharge from the eyes or painful eyes which is indicated by increased blinking and holding the eyes shut. Eye problems caused by cat flu are especially serious in cats with short noses such as Persians or Himalayans (see Eye Problems on page 95).

Like most viral infections the best treatment is supportive care while the infection takes its course over three to seven days. More severe or complicated infections will require treatments like fluid support, antibiotics, antiviral medication and treatment for eye ulcers. If your cat has a history of episodes of cat flu, or if you suspect that it may have cat flu it is reasonable to start supportive care.

Supportive treatment for cat flu includes humidifying the air your cat breathes three to six times per day. Ideally you can do this using a nebuliser with saline. If you do not have a nebuliser you can simply put your cat in a steamy bathroom while someone is having a hot shower. You should also offer various strong smelling or warmed foods (see Reduced Appetite and Anorexia on page 61). You can also try to increase its water intake. Wet foods are better because they increase water intake. You can also add water to the cat's food to increase water intake. Adding a sprinkle of salt to its water may encourage it to drink; however, you should not do this if your cat has been diagnosed with heart or kidney problems. Adding a few drops of brine from a tin of tuna to its water bowl may help encourage water intake. If your cat is not at all interested in food and water you can try to carefully syringe either some pureed food, water or a balanced electrolyte solution into its mouth. Most cats will require around 200–250 mL water per day from their food and drinking water.

If your cat becomes overly depressed, is not eating well for 48 hours or if it is having difficulty breathing you should take it to see your veterinarian. If the nasal discharge becomes yellow or green your cat may benefit from antibiotics and you should take your cat to your veterinarian. Similarly all eye problems can be very serious (see Eye Problems on page 95). If you suspect that your cat has an eye problem you should take it to your veterinarian.

Other causes of sneezing, sniffling, snuffling, nasal discharge or noisy breathing can be more serious and are often long-term or recurrent problems over weeks to months. Cats do not like breathing through their mouth so anything blocking their nose can cause severe difficulty breathing. If this is the case or if your cat is breathing through its mouth, you should take it to see your veterinarian. Some causes of nasal problems in cats other than cat flu will only affect one nostril and in this case you should take your cat to your veterinarian.

Scabs, sores and lumps on the nose can indicate dermatitis or tumours called squamous cell carcinomas due to sun exposure. These are most likely to occur on unpigmented skin. These can be serious and progressive but early treatment can be very effective. These tumours can also affect unpigmented eyelids or the tips of the ears.

Eye Problems

Cats can develop problems with their eyes for several reasons. Possibilities include an infection with cat flu (see Sneezing, Sniffles and Snuffles on page 92) and injuries such as lacerations sustained in a fight with another cat. They can also result from being hit by a car, objects stuck in the eye or irritant poisons or stink bug (also known as bronze orange, shield, green shield or green vegetable bugs) spray in the eye. Sometimes a disease affecting the rest of the body will manifest as a problem with the eyes.

Yellow or green discharge from the eye may indicate an infection. Changes in the appearance of the eyes can indicate a problem. Such changes include a change in the size of the pupils or uneven pupil size. Other indications are cloudiness or a bluish tinge to the eyes, filling with blood, redness or swelling of the tissues around the eyes including the conjunctiva and eyelids or bulging of the eyes. Signs of eye pain include an increased rate of blinking or holding the eyes shut. Cats with painful eyes will often not like being in overly bright areas and may appear scared of light. They may also appear head shy and not like their head being touched or approached.

Cats with high blood pressure can bleed into their retinas (the light sensors at the back of the eyes). In more extreme circumstances the retinas can become detached due to high blood pressure. This can result in sudden blindness, which is seen as dilated pupils, confusion, agitation and distress. If your cat has suddenly become blind you should take it to see your veterinarian immediately.

Cats with short noses such as Himalayans, Persians and Chinchillas are more prone to problems with the surface of their eyes (the cornea) because they are more exposed. Burmese cats can have high blood fat levels and can be prone to the eyes becoming suddenly clouded with fat, but this condition can potentially occur in any cat.

If your cat's eyes become contaminated with an irritating toxin you should flush them out with large amounts of tepid water or saline for 10–20 minutes then seek veterinary attention for your cat as soon as possible. Also call a poisons information service for specific advice regarding the particular toxin involved. Stink bug sprays are foul smelling, very irritating and can cause severe ulceration to the surface of the eye. There are several varieties of stink bug, known by names such as: bronze orange bug, shield bug, green shield bug or green vegetable bug. These are all shield-shaped and range from dark bronze or orange to apple or jade green in colour or may simply be brown. They are found on the east coast of Australia, in Britain, New Zealand, Japan, throughout the Americas and on Pacific Islands. They feed on a wide variety of crops, often occur where citrus trees are found and are most common in spring and summer. The bugs release their spray when frightened or disturbed. The eye will be intensely painful and the cat will hold the eye shut. The eye may become swollen and inflamed. If you suspect that you cat has suffered a stink bug spray in its eye, the affected eye should be flushed as for any other toxin and you should take your cat to your veterinarian.

The eyes are very delicate and precious. Any problem with the eyes is potentially an emergency and time is of the essence. Timely treatment is vital with eye problems to avoid long-term problems like blindness. Regardless of the cause of the problem, applying artificial or synthetic tears regularly may be of benefit and will not be detrimental. When applying artificial tears, using a different tube for each eye can help reduce cross contamination between the eyes with irritant substances and infectious agents.

Diabetes

Diabetes mellitus or sugar diabetes is a relatively common condition in older cats and causes numerous health complications including an increased susceptibility to infections. The first sign of diabetes is usually increased thirst and increased urination. Affected animals may have increased appetite but lose weight. Your cat may also be lethargic. In advanced stages cats with diabetes may start to walk on their hocks, which is called a plantigrade stance. Cats with diabetes are also much more sensitive to other illnesses and can become very sick quite quickly. This is especially true when the illness causes a poor appetite or vomiting. A diabetic cat can deteriorate quickly, so if it is unwell you should take it to your veterinarian as soon as possible.

A cat walking normally.

A diabetic cat with a plantigrade stance.

Cats are unique animals; they are the only non-primate animals that get Type 2 diabetes. Because cats are secretive, by the time their diabetes is diagnosed the diabetes has advanced and they are usually considered insulin dependent. Sometimes feline diabetes can be managed with diet and oral glucose-controlling medication. Another consideration with feline diabetes is that it can sometimes be cured with treatment or can be transient. This means that at times a cat may be diabetic and insulin dependent but at other times it may not be diabetic at all. The importance of this is that diabetic cats' insulin requirements can vary and they need to be monitored closely.

Low blood sugar (hypoglycaemia)

Often diabetic cats are treated with insulin to lower their blood glucose and help control the disease. One of the most common complications of insulin treatment is low blood sugar or hypoglycaemia. Signs of hypoglycaemia include crankiness and agitation, laziness, weakness, incoordination, a head tilt, circling, twitching, collapse and possibly convulsions.

Hypoglycaemia can be caused by an excess of insulin. One cause of this is an inadvertent insulin overdose. This is usually either a ten times overdose or a two times overdose. A ten times overdose usually occurs when a person not properly trained with insulin administration misreads the syringe and draws up ten times the dose of insulin. Two times insulin overdoses usually occur when two different carers each give the cat its insulin injection. Make sure that everyone giving the injections knows exactly how to do it. Occasionally an insulin overdose occurs if the wrong insulin syringe is used with the wrong insulin. Always ensure that you use the correct syringes. Sometimes weight loss, a poor appetite, a change in diet or another drug being stopped affects a cat's insulin requirement. Diabetes in cats can be transitory so their insulin requirement can become reduced spontaneously. In these cases even their normal dose may cause a problem.

If your cat starts to show signs of hypoglycaemia, you should feed it a meal. If your cat seems to recover continue to feed it small meals every 1–2 hours at least until it is next due for insulin. Your veterinarian may have given you specific advice regarding the insulin dose in this situation. If you have not been given any specific guidelines on what to do if your cat shows mild signs of hypoglycaemia you should call your veterinarian. If you are unable to contact your veterinarian and your cat is eating well and is otherwise bright, the safest thing is to skip one dose of insulin and contact your veterinarian as soon as possible for advice regarding starting the insulin again. It is not safe to delay seeking veterinary attention if your diabetic cat is not eating well or is sick. The guidelines that your veterinarian gives you may also involve using urine test strips that can detect glucose in the urine or a glucometer to measure the glucose in the blood. When reading urine test strips it is important to follow the instructions on the packet exactly.

If your cat collapses or starts seizuring, rub some honey or another sweet liquid such as corn syrup on its gums. Do this carefully to avoid being bitten. Do not pour anything into your cat's mouth as it may choke. This treatment will usually be effective in 1–2 minutes. Once your cat has recovered you should feed it something then take it to your veterinarian. The meal should ideally be high in protein, such as cat food or meat but you can give it whatever it will eat. If it does not recover within two minutes rub more honey or other sugary solution into its gums and take your cat to your veterinarian.

Hypoglycaemia, caused by accidental insulin overdose, can be very severe. If you realise your cat has received an insulin overdose you should feed it a meal and take it to your veterinarian immediately. Take some honey or sweet liquid with you in case it collapses or starts seizuring on the way.

Ketosis

If your diabetic cat is not eating well or is vomiting and unwell, it is at risk of developing hypoglycaemia. You may have been given advice on what to do with the insulin dose on days when it is not eating well. If you have to alter the insulin dose for more than 24–36 hours this probably indicates a more serious problem which needs to be investigated by your veterinarian. Diabetic cats which are unwell are also at risk of developing, or may already have a condition called ketosis (also known as diabetic ketoacidosis or DKA for short). This condition usually occurs because the cat has another illness making them unwell, such as a urinary tract infection or pancreatitis in addition to the diabetes. These cats are especially at risk if they are getting less or no insulin because you are concerned about causing hypoglycaemia due to a poor appetite or vomiting. Diabetic cats are at risk of both hypoglycaemia and prolonged hyperglycaemia.

During ketosis, fat breaks down and toxic byproducts build up. These cause the cat to have a distinctive acetone smell to their breath. Some people are especially good at detecting ketotic breath while others find it much harder. Your veterinarian may give you urine test strips to detect ketones in the urine. Any ketones in the urine are abnormal. When reading urine test strips it is import to follow the instructions on the packet exactly. Sometimes ketosis develops in diabetic cats that have not yet been diagnosed and so are not receiving treatment. Ketosis is a very serious condition which can make diabetic cats very unwell and can be fatal. If you suspect that your cat has ketosis, you should take it to your veterinarian as soon as possible.

Kidney Problems

Cats can develop kidney or renal problems including kidney or renal insufficiency or failure for many reasons. In older cats the most common form of this is chronic renal insufficiency. This occurs gradually over a long period of time through progressive degeneration of the kidneys. Eventually there is insufficient kidney function to concentrate the urine or to prevent poisons building up, which the kidneys usually excrete. Cats can still cope to a point, even if their kidneys are not functioning sufficiently. However, cats with kidney problems (kidney or renal insufficiency or failure) are prone to complications such as dehydration, constipation, oral and stomach ulcers, high blood pressure and urinary tract infections. Cats can also develop kidney or renal insufficiency or acute failure, such as with lily or antifreeze (ethylene glycol) toxicity, which usually cause a rapidly progressive and serious illness (see Poisoning on page 74).

The major signs of kidney problems (kidney or renal insufficiency or failure) include increased drinking and urination. There may be weight loss and the coat may develop an unkept appearance. Affected cats may have bad breath due to a build-up of poisons in their body. They often have reduced appetites and may vomit. There may be evidence of bleeding into the stomach, seen as flecks of fresh blood, a tinge of blood or digested blood that looks like coffee grounds in the vomit. Their faeces may also become black. Over time their gums may become very pale rather than a healthy pink colour. Cats with kidney problems are prone to dehydration (see Dehydration on page 64). Cats with kidney problems are also sensitive to changes in salt intake so they should not be given overly salty foods or have salt added to their drinking water. Dehydration can lead to constipation (see page 65). High blood pressure associated with kidney problems can lead to damage or detachment of the retinas (the light sensors at the back of the eyes) which can lead to sudden blindness (see

Eye Problems on page 95). Cats with kidney problems are at increased risk of developing a urinary tract infection. Signs of a urinary tract infection include increased frequency of urination, straining to urinate and bloody or smelly urine (see Lower Urinary Problems on page 70). Urinary tract infections can cause cats, that are coping well with their chronic kidney problems, to become unwell.

Cats with kidney problems are not as good at coping with other illnesses as healthy cats and can quickly become dehydrated and very unwell. If your cat has kidney problems and is unwell, you should take it to your veterinarian promptly before it becomes seriously unwell.

Heart Disease

Cats can have heart problems from birth (congenital) or they can acquire them. The most common cause of acquired heart disease in cats is a group of problems with the heart muscle or cardiomyopathies. The causes of these problems are largely unknown. Occasionally one of these conditions, dilated cardiomyopathy, is caused by a diet deficient in taurine. Providing additional taurine may help reverse this condition. Almost all commercial diets now have ample quantities of taurine so this has become a very rare form of heart disease. Cardiomyopathies can lead to congestive heart failure, fainting or episodic weakness and to the formation of blood clots. These are all very serious signs and necessitate veterinary attention.

Cats with certain types of heart disease can have episodes of weakness or collapse. Often cats will recover very quickly from this. However, any cause of weakness is always serious and you should take your cat to your veterinarian if you notice weakness.

When the heart starts to fail and cannot pump enough blood, there may be water and salt retention. Eventually the heart becomes unable to deal with the fluid so the fluid either builds up in the abdomen or more commonly in or around the lungs. This is known as congestive heart failure. Fluid in or around the lungs causes difficulty breathing and low blood oxygen levels that can cause a bluish tinge to the gums. Difficulty breathing is always an emergency and if your cat is having difficulty breathing you should keep it as calm as possible and take it to see your veterinarian as soon as possible. If your cat is on long-term therapy for heart disease, you may have been given instructions to administer additional diuretics if there are signs of congestive heart failure. Cats in congestive heart failure will also often be hypothermic (see Hypothermia on page 67). You can carefully try to warm your cat up while you transport it to your veterinarian. However, sometimes cats in congestive heart failure will be very agitated and not tolerate being warmed so you should not stress them. Cats in congestive heart failure are in a very serious condition and any additional stress can kill them.

When the heart becomes very diseased some of the chambers of the heart (the left atrium) become very dilated. This causes areas of blood within the chamber to be stagnant and other areas where the blood flow is very turbulent. These conditions increase the risk of blood clots forming. These blood clots may leave the heart and block the blood supply to one or more of the limbs or other parts of the body. Blood clots most commonly lodge in the blood vessels supplying the hind limbs causing hind limb weakness or paralysis. However, the blood supply to either of the forelimbs, the brain or the lungs can also be affected. Affected limbs will be weak, cold or paralysed and they may be very painful. With time the muscles in the limbs may become very hard and swollen. Sometimes cats with blood clots will also be in congestive heart failure concurrently. Blood clots are very serious complications of heart disease and if you suspect that your cat has one you should take it to your veterinarian immediately.

Cats being treated with diuretics which stop eating for any reason are at risk of becoming dehydrated or developing electrolyte imbalances. The difficulty is that it is dangerous to stop diuretic therapy suddenly because it can result in congestive heart failure. If your cat is on diuretic therapy and stops eating you should take it to see your veterinarian.

Hyperthyroidism

Hyperthyroidism is a relatively common hormonal abnormality in older cats. It is caused by an overactive thyroid gland causing increased levels of thyroid hormone. The thyroid gland is located in the neck and the change in this is usually not cancerous. The increased level of thyroid hormone has effects on all parts of the body. It drastically increases the metabolic rate and causes weight loss despite an increased appetite. Due to the increased food intake the stools will often also be very large. Sometimes affected cats will vomit. Cats with hyperthyroidism will often have an unkempt coat. Usually cats with hyperthyroidism will be hyperactive, very irritable and cranky. Occasionally affected cats will instead become quite and have a reduced appetite. Hyperthyroidism can cause detrimental effects on the heart and the kidneys. If the disease has become advanced, this can be severe. Cats with hyperthyroidism often drink and urinate excessively.

Hyperthyroidism is rarely an emergency unless it is very severe and causes heart problems (see Heart Disease on page 101 and Kidney Problems on page 100). When hyperthyroidism is severe and causes collapse it is known as thyroid storm and if you suspect that your cat has this you should take it to your veterinarian as soon as possible.

If you suspect that your cat has hyperthyroidism you should take it to your veterinarian to have this investigated. There are several treatment options for hyperthyroidism including medical, radioactive iodine treatment and surgical options. All medications can have side effects. If your cat is being treated medically for hyperthyroidism you should ask you veterinarians about possible side effects so that you know what to look for and how often it should be monitored.

Queening (Labour)

Cats are usually good mothers and labour and birth is usually fairly smooth. You or your veterinarian rarely need to intervene. However, it can be detrimental to both kittens and queen to delay taking a queen having birthing difficulties to a veterinarian. This chapter provides some guidelines on how to identify when there is a problem with the birthing process.

The average duration of a cat's pregnancy is 66 days from the date of mating. Not all matings will result in a pregnancy and cats can maintain a normal figure until late in the pregnancy so pregnancy should be confirmed by your veterinarian. A day or so before giving birth, a queen may undergo several behavioural changes. She may eat less and find a quiet place to give birth such as a cupboard or under a bed. It is generally accepted that a queen's rectal temperature may drop below 37.8°C 12–36 hours before labour. Leading up to queening you should check your cat's temperature three times a day. Make these measurements at the same time each day. If you notice a temperature drop, usually below 37.8°C, you should compare this to the average of the previous week's temperature measurements. If the drop is 0.7–1°C, labour may follow in the next 12–24 hours. However, this is not always completely reliable and sometimes labour does not follow. Regardless, if kittening has not occurred within 36 hours after a temperature drop you should see your veterinarian to investigate this. Milk may be expressed from the nipples 24–48 hours before queening.

If you suspect that your queen is pregnant, you should definitely take your queen to a veterinarian if it is greater than 69 days from mating and there are no signs of labour.

The entire kittening process usually takes 2–12 hours. Occasionally it will take much longer, especially if the queen is interrupted and the process is stopped. During the first stage of labour the queen will be restless and frequently pace, groom and may vocalise. She may even vomit. During this time no abdominal or uterine contractions are evident. A poor appetite and occasional vomiting is not a reason to be concerned unless the vomiting is excessive or the queen is weak or in pain. Just before giving birth, the nesting behaviour may intensify and the queen may start to purr loudly. If she has not given birth to any kittens after 12 hours of this behaviour you should take your queen to your veterinarian.

The second stage of labour involves dilation of the cervix and passage of the kittens. Before each kitten clear fluid may be passed. This is often followed by green, black, red or brown discharge. Kittens may be passed within minutes of each other but they may be up to 30–60 minutes apart. Difficulty passing kittens is rare but if there is active straining or strong abdominal contractions and a kitten is not passed within 30 minutes to 1 hour this indicates a problem. Similarly, 1–2 hours of weak, infrequent straining without producing a kitten may also indicate a problem. If any of these situations occur, and you feel comfortable doing so, you can put on some examination gloves and with lots of lubrication, gently examine the vulva by parting the labia. If you can see a kitten you can gently try to help it out. Do this by gently pulling on the kitten in a slightly downwards direction. Only put gentle traction on the kitten when the queen is contracting. Do not pull on the kitten's head or neck, instead gently pull from its body or limbs. If you are having difficulty gripping the kitten, using a towel to hold it may help. If either there is no kitten visible or you cannot gently dislodge it within 5–10 minutes you should take the queen and the other kittens to your veterinarian.

It is not unusual for kittens to come out back feet first (breech position). This is not abnormal and usually not a problem.

The queen usually licks off the foetal membranes that cover the kittens and breaks the umbilical cord. This helps stimulate breathing in the kittens. Once a kitten has been born, if the queen has not removed these membranes within 1–3 minutes you should intervene by laying the kitten on a soft towel and rubbing it vigorously but gently with another towel to remove these membranes. You should use a fresh towel for each kitten. If the kitten's mouth and nose is full of fluid you can use a syringe to gently suck it out or a piece of cloth to wipe it up. You can also cup a kitten in your hands with the head at your fingertips and the tail towards your wrist and then gently swing the kitten up and down as if you were chopping wood (see picture below). You should, of course, be careful not to let go of the kitten or jar it. If your hands are big enough, you can hold the kitten's body in one hand and use your index finger over the kitten's head to stop it leaving your hand (see picture below). You can then swing the kitten by gently lifting it up and swinging it downwards four or five times. This helps to remove fluid from the airways and stimulates breathing.

If a kitten is still not breathing, you can continue to rub it for another one minute to try to stimulate its breathing. If the kitten is still not breathing after this you should give it five tiny breaths through its nose while holding its mouth shut. Be careful that the breaths are not too big or forceful as you could damage the tiny lungs. You should then check if it has a heartbeat by feeling its chest. If it does not have a heartbeat, you should start very gentle CPR as discussed in Cardiopulmonary Resuscitation (CPR) on page 42. Do not give up easily as occasionally it may take one to two hours for a kitten to start breathing for itself. However, remember that you also have to look after the queen and the other kittens.

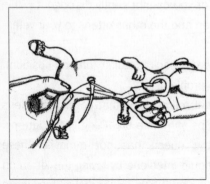

Tying off and cutting the umbilical cord.

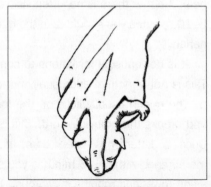

Carefully cleaning a kitten's airway.

If your cat is ever in pain, weak or collapsed during queening you should take her to your veterinarian.

The queen usually breaks the umbilical cord with her teeth. If she does not do this you will have to tie it off and cut it. You should use some fine thread to tie a tight knot around the umbilical cord about 3 centimetres away from the kitten's belly. Then place a second knot 2 centimetres further away from this. You can then cut between these two knots. You should then dip the severed ends of the umbilical cord in an iodine solution such as Betadine®. Be careful not to pull on the umbilical cord as this can cause a hernia. It is important to ensure that the kittens do not become tangled in each other's umbilical cords as this can hurt or strangle them. Similarly it is important to ensure that a kitten's umbilical cord does not become wrapped around its legs.

Not every kitten will be followed by a placenta and sometimes two kittens will be passed before either of their placentas is passed. It is useful to try to ensure that as many placentas as kittens have been passed because retained placentas can cause problems. This can be difficult because it is natural for the queen to eat the placentas. If this is the case do not worry about accounting for all the placentas too much.

Green, black, red or brown vulval discharge in the absence of other signs of labour can indicate a problem and is another reason to take your queen to your veterinarian.

If your cat is lethargic, anorexic or does not seem to have the normal mothering instincts and is not nursing the kittens well, she may be unwell and should see your veterinarian. Similarly if there is excessive or continued bleeding from the vulva she should see your veterinarian. If the discharge from the vulva becomes yellow or creamy or foul smelling this may indicate a uterine infection and she should see your veterinarian immediately. When taking a queen to your veterinarian, always take the kittens with you.

Emergency Contacts

Australia

EMERGENCY—Police, Fire, Ambulance: 000

Poisons Information Centre: 131 126

Local Council Ranger phone:. . . . . After-hours: . . . .

United Kingdom

EMERGENCY—Police, Fire, Ambulance: 999

For Poisons Information contact the RSPCA

RSPCA 24-hour: 0870 555 5999

Council Animal welfare phone: . . . . After-hours: . . . .

New Zealand

EMERGENCY—Police, Fire, Ambulance: 111

National Poison Centre: 0800 764 766

Royal NZ SPCA: 09 827 6094

Local Council Ranger phone:. . . . . After-hours: . . . .

Veterinary clinic name:. . . . .

Veterinarian's name: . . . .

Phone: . . . . Opening hours: . . . .

Address:. . . . .

. . . .

Emergency Veterinary clinic 1 . . . .

Phone: . . . . Opening hours: . . . .

Address:. . . . .

. . . .

Emergency Veterinary clinic 2 . . . .

Phone: . . . . Opening hours: . . . .

Address:. . . . .

. . . .

Your Cat's Health History

Vaccinations, Intestinal Worming, Flea Control, Results of Routine Check-ups, etc.

Date: . . . .   Comments: . . . .

Date: . . . .   Comments: . . . .

Date: . . . .   Comments: . . . .

Date: . . . .   Comments: . . . .

Date: . . . .   Comments: . . . .

Date: . . . .   Comments: . . . .

Date: . . . .   Comments: . . . .

Date: . . . .   Comments: . . . .

Date: . . . .   Comments: . . . .

Date: . . . .   Comments: . . . .

Date: . . . .   Comments: . . . .

Date: . . . .   Comments: . . . .

Date: . . . .   Comments: . . . .

Date: . . . .   Comments: . . . .

Date: . . . .   Comments: . . . .

Date: . . . .   Comments: . . . .

Date: . . . .   Comments: . . . .

Date: . . . .   Comments: . . . .

Date: . . . .   Comments: . . . .

Date: . . . .   Comments: . . . .

Date: . . . .   Comments: . . . .

Date: . . . .   Comments: . . . .

Date: . . . .   Comments: . . . .

Date: . . . .   Comments: . . . .

Date: . . . .   Comments: . . . .

Date: . . . .   Comments: . . . .

Date: . . . .   Comments: . . . .